HASPELS ADDENDA
Additional References to C. H. E. Haspels
Attic Black-figured Lekythoi

HASPELS ADDENDA

Additional References to
C. H. E. Haspels
Attic Black-figured Lekythoi

Compiled by
T. Mannack

AT THE BEAZLEY ARCHIVE

Published for THE BRITISH ACADEMY
by OXFORD UNIVERSITY PRESS

Oxford University Press, Great Clarendon Street, Oxford OX2 6DP

Oxford New York
Auckland Cape Town Dar es Salaam Hong Kong Karachi
Kuala Lumpur Madrid Melbourne Mexico City Nairobi
New Delhi Shanghai Taipei Toronto

With offices in
Argentina Austria Brazil Chile Czech Republic France Greece
Guatemala Hungary Italy Japan Poland Portugal Singapore
South Korea Switzerland Thailand Turkey Ukraine Vietnam

Published in the United States
by Oxford University Press Inc., New York

British Library Cataloguing in Publication Data
Data available

Library of Congress in Publication Data
Data available

Typeset by J&L Composition, Filey, North Yorkshire
Printed in Great Britain
on acid-free paper by
The Cromwell Press Limited
Trowbridge, Wilts

ISBN 0-19-726315-1 978-0-19-726315-0

Contents

Preface

Caroline Henriette Emilie Haspels was born in 1894 at Colmschate in the Netherlands. She studied Classics at the Municipal University of Amsterdam, and chose Classical Archaeology as one of the options for the final examinations in 1923. Her teacher was Jan Six. Scholarships enabled Miss Haspels to enrol as a postgraduate student at Utrecht University, and to spend several months at the universities of Oxford and Munich. At Oxford, in 1928 and 1930, she was instructed by Professor J. D. Beazley, in Munich, in 1929, by Ernst Buschor. In 1935 Miss Haspels submitted her doctoral thesis, *Bijdrage tot de studie van Attisch Zwartfigurig*. It was published by the French Institute at Athens with the title *Attic Black-Figured Lekythoi* (1936).

This volume of *Addenda* to C. H. E. Haspels, *ABL* was promised in 1989 (*Beazley Addenda*², xi). It was originally intended to include additional information to Miss Haspels' lists in the second edition of *Beazley Addenda*. However, since Beazley did not incorporate her work in his lists, *ABL* has been a distinct entity, and a separate list of *Addenda* is therefore more useful for scholars. The format is that of *Beazley Addenda*: we have endeavoured to include all new references to illustrations of the more than 1,500 vases listed by Miss Haspels in books and periodicals received by the Sackler Library (formerly the Ashmolean Library). In addition, we have also included references to vases added by Sir John Beazley in *ABV* and *Paralipomena* to Professor Haspels' lists.

Like *Beazley Addenda*, *Haspels Addenda* is based on the Beazley Archive's database of Athenian black- and red-figure vases, which was inaugurated by the Beazley Archivist, Professor Donna Kurtz, and the Lincoln Professor of Art and Archaeology, Sir John Boardman, in 1979. Reviewers have justly drawn attention to numerous shortcomings in the two editions of *Beazley Addenda*, and many may have found their way into this volume. Financial constraints have reduced the staff of the Beazley Archive's pottery database to a single researcher. He has been very grateful for any help. Any additions and corrections will be most welcome, and will be added to the Beazley Archive's pottery database. This will be the last printed version of any *Addenda*. In future, new references to published pictures and profile drawings will be added to the database, which is available on the world wide web (www.beazley.ox.ac.uk).

Publication has been made possible by the generous support of the British Academy. The Beazley Archive's technical director, Greg Parker, has written the programme to extract the relevant information from the database. Eleni

Hatzivassiliou has kindly made many corrections and additions to the manuscript. Last but not least I would like to thank the staff of the Sackler Library for their help and their patience, in particular Jane Bruder, Henri Coles, and James McBain.

Abbreviations

150 Jahre Antikensammlungen *150 Jahre Antikensammlungen in Karlsruhe, Badisches Landesmuseum 1838–1988.*

ABV Beazley, J. D., *Attic Black-Figure Vase-Painters* (Oxford, 1956).

Acta *Acta Praehistorica et Archeologica* 34 (2002).

Acta Hungaricae *Acta Antiquaria Academiae Scientiarum Hungaricae* 41 (2001).

Acta Upsaliensis *Acta Universitatis Upsaliensis. From the Gustavianum Collections in Uppsala* 2 (1978).

ADelt *Archaiologikon Deltion* 50 (1995).

Ahlberg-Cornell, *Herakles* Ahlberg-Cornell, G., *Herakles and the Sea-Monster in Attic Black-Figure Vase-Painting* (Stockholm, 1984).

Ahlberg-Cornell, *Myth* Ahlberg-Cornell, G., *Myth and Epos in Early Greek Art, Representation and Interpretation* (Jonsered, 1992).

AJA *American Journal of Archaeology* 105 (2001).

AK *Antike Kunst* 45 (2002).

Aktseli, *Altäre* Aktseli, D., *Altäre in der archaischen und klassischen Kunst, Untersuchungen zu Typologie und Ikonographie* (Espelkamp, 1996).

AM *Mitteilungen des Deutschen Archäologischen Instituts, Athenische Abteilung* 116 (2001).

Anderson, *Hunting* Anderson, J., *Hunting in the Ancient World* (Berkeley, 1985).

Anderson & West Anderson, J. & West, K. (eds.), *Poseidon's Realm* (Crocker Art Museum, Sacramento, 1982).

Andreae, *Ulisse* Andreae, B. *et al.*, *Ulisse, il mito e la memoria* (Rome, 1996).

Andreassi, *Jatta di Ruvo* Andreassi, G., *Jatta di Ruvo, la famiglia, la collezione, il Museo Nazionale* (Bari, 1996).

Angeli, *Hallstattkultur* Angeli, W., *et al.*, *Die Hallstattkultur, Frühform europäischer Einheit, Internationale Ausstellung des Landes Oberösterreich 25.* April bis 26.Okt. (Linz, 1980).

Angiolillo, *Pisistrato* Angiolillo, S., *Arte e cultura nell'Atene di Pisistrato e dei Pisistratidi* (Bari, 1997).

Annali *Annali del Seminario di Studi del Mondo Classico* 6 (1999).

AntClass *L'Antiquité classique* 69 (2000).

Anz *Archäologischer Anzeiger* (2001).

Archaic Greek Art Charbonneaux, J., Martin, R., and Villard, F., *Archaic Greek Art* (London, 1971).

Archeo *Archeo, Attualita di Passato.*

Arias & Hirmer Arias, P. & Hirmer, M., *A History of Greek Vase Painting* (London, 1962).

Arrigoni, *Donne* Arrigoni, G. (ed.), *Le donne in Grecia* (Bari, 1985).

Arte Griego Barbera, J., and Sanmarti, E., *Arte Griego en Espana* (Barcelona, 1987).

*ARV*² Beazley, J.D., *Attic Red-Figure Vase-Painters, 2nd edn.* (Oxford, 1963).
Aspects of Ancient Greece Allentown Art Museum, Ferrari Pinney, G., Ridgway, B. S., *Aspects of Ancient Greece, Pennsylvania* (16.9–30.12.1979).
Ausgestellte Werke Heilmeyer, W-D., *et al., Antikenmuseum Berlin, Die ausgestellten Werke* (Berlin, 1988).

BABesch Bulletin van de Vereeniging tot Bevordering der Kennis van de Antieke Beschaving tes Gravenhage 76 (2001).
BAdd Carpenter, T. H., with Mannack, T., and Mendonca, M., *Beazley Addenda*, 2nd edn. (Oxford, 1989).
Balty, *Animaux* Balty, J., et al., *Des animaux et des hommes, témoignages de la Préhistoire et de l'Antiquité* (Brussels, 1988).
Barresi and Valastro Barresi, S. and Valastro, S., *Vasi attici figurati vasi sicelioti, Museo civico di Castello Ursino* (Catania, 2000).
Barringer, *Devine Escorts* Barringer, J. M., *Divine Escorts, Nereids in Archaic and Classical Greek Art* (Ann Arbor, 1995).
Bastet, *Rottiers* Bastet, F. L., *De drie collecties Rottiers te Leiden* (Leiden, 1991).
Baumeister, *Denkmäler* Baumeister, A., (ed.), *Denkmäler des klassischen Altertums*, I–II (Munich, 1885–88).
BdA Bollettino d'Arte 117 (2001).
Beck, *Album* Beck, F., *Album of Greek Education* (Sydney, 1975).
Berard, *Anodoi* Berard, D., *Anodoi* (Rome, 1974).
Berard, *Image* Berard, C., *L'Image de l'autre et le Héros Etranger, Sciences et Racisme* (Lausanne, 1986).
Berard, *Images et société* Berard, C. (ed.), *Images et société en Grèce ancienne, L'iconographie comme méthode d'analyse, Cahiers d'Archeologie Romande* 36 (Lausanne, 1987).
Bernhard-Walcher, *Antikes Leben* Bernhard-Walcher, A., *Alltag, Feste, Religion, Antikes Leben auf griechischen Vasen, eine Ausstellung des Kunsthistorischen Museums* (Vienna, 1991).
Berti and Gasparri Berti, F. and Gasparri, C., *Dionysos, mito e mistero* (Bologna, 1989).
Berti and Restani, *musica* Berti, F., and Restani, D. (eds.), *Lo specchio della musica, iconografia nella ceramica attica di Spina* (Bologna, 1988).
Berti and Guzzo Berti, F., and Guzzo, P. G. (eds.), *Spina, Storia di una citta tra Greci ed Etruschi* (Ferrara, 1993).
Bestattungswesen Horst, F., and Keiling, H. (eds.), *Bestattungswesen und Totenkult in ur- und frühgeschichtlicher Zeit* (Berlin, 1991).
BICS Bulletin of the Institute of Classical Studies 45 (2001).
Bieber, *Theater* Bieber, M., *The History of the Greek and Roman Theater,* 2nd edn. (Princeton, 1961).
Birchler Emery, *Musique* Birchler Emery, P. *et al., La musique et la danse dans l'Antiquité, Regards sur les collections du Musée d'art et d'histoire de Genève* (Geneva, 1996).
Blok, *Early Amazons* Blok, J. H., *The Early Amazons, Modern and Ancient Perspectives on a Persistent Myth* (Leiden, 1995).
BMY British Museum Yearbook 4 (1980).
Boardman, *ABFV* Boardman, J., *Athenian Black Figure Vases* (London, 1974).
Boardman, *Ceramica* Boardman, J., (ed.), *La ceramica antica* (Milan, 1984).

Boardman, *Classical* Boardman, J., *Athenian Red Figure Vases, The Classical Period* (London, 1989).

Boardman, *Greeks Overseas* Boardman, J., *The Greeks Overseas,* 4th edn. (London, 1999).

Boardman, *History* Boardman, J., *The History of Greek vases, potters, painters and pictures* (London, 2001).

Bol, *Liebieghaus* Bol, P., *Frankfurt am Main, Liebieghaus, Führer durch die Sammlungen; Antike Kunst* (Frankfurt, 1980).

Bonacasa, *Stile Severo* Bonacasa, N. (ed.), *Lo Stile Severo in Grecia e in Occidente, Aspetti e problemi, Studi e Materiali* 9 (Rome, 1995).

Bothmer, *Amazons* Bothmer, D. von, *Amazons in Greek Art* (Oxford, 1957).

Bothmer, *Bastis* Bothmer, B. v. *et al., Antiquities from the Collection of Christos G. Bastis* (Mainz, 1987).

Brijder, *Proceedings* Brijder, H., *Ancient Greek and Related Pottery, Proceedings of Vase Symposium* (Amsterdam, 1984).

Brinkmann, *Beobachtungen* Brinkmann, V., *Beobachtungen zum formalen Aufbau und zum Sinngehalt der Friese des Siphnierschatzhauses* (Ennepetal, 1994).

Brize, *Geryoneis* Brize, P., *Geryoneis des Stesichoros und die frühe griechische Kunst* (Würzburg, 1980).

Brommer, *Heracles* Brommer, F., *Heracles, The Twelve Labors of the Hero in Ancient Art and Literature* (Translation, New York, 1986).

Brommer, *Herakles* Brommer, F., *Herakles,* 2nd edn. (Köln, 1972).

Brommer, *Herakles II* Brommer, F., *Herakles II* (Darmstadt, 1984).

Brommer, *Odysseus* Brommer, F., *Odysseus* (Darmstadt, 1983).

Brommer, *Satyrspiele* Brommer, F., *Satyrspiele,* 2nd edn. (Berlin, 1959).

Buitron, *New England* Buitron, D., *Attic Vase Painting in New England Collections* (Cambridge, Mass., 1972).

Buitron, *Odyssey* Buitron, D., *The Odyssey and ancient art, an epic in word and image* (New York, 1992).

Buitron-Oliver, *Douris* Buitron-Oliver, D., *Douris, A Master-Painter of Athenian Red-Figure Vases* (Mainz, 1995).

Buitron-Oliver, *New Perspectives* Buitron-Oliver, D. (ed.), *New Perspectives in Early Greek Art* (Hanover and London, 1991).

BullMetMus *Bulletin of the Metropolitan Museum of Art, New York* (Winter 2000).

BullMich *Bulletin, Museums of Art and Archaeology, University of Michigan* 13 (2000/1).

Burke & Pollitt Burke, S. & Pollit, J., *Greek Vases at Yale* (New Haven, 1975).

Buschor, *Satyrtänze* Buschor, E., *Satyrtänze und frühes Drama* (Munich, 1943).

Buschor, *Jenseits* Buschor, E., *Die Musen des Jenseits* (Munich, 1944).

Buxton, *Grèce imaginaire* Buxton, R., *La grèce de l'imaginaire, les contextes de la mythologie* (Paris, 1996).

CAH *Cambridge Ancient History.*

Callipolitis-Feytmans Callipolitis-Feytmans, D., *Plats attiques a figures noires* (Paris, 1974).

Cambitoglou, *Nicholson Museum* Cambitoglou, A. (ed.), *Classical Art in the Nicholson Museum, Sydney* (Mainz, 1995).

Carpenter, *Art and Myth* Carpenter, T.H., *Art and Myth in Ancient Greece* (London, 1991).

Carpenter, *Fifth-Century Imagery* Carpenter, T. H., *Dionysian Imagery in Fifth-Century Athens* (Oxford, 1997).

Cavalier, *Silence et Fureur* Cavalier, O. (ed.), *Silence et Fureur, La femme et le marriage en Grèce, Les antiquités grecques du Musée Calvet* (Avignon, ca.1997).

Ceccarelli, *Pirrica* Ceccarelli, P., *La pirrica nell'antichità greco romana, studi sulla danza armata* (Pisa, 1998).

Centaur's Smile Padgett, M., *The Centaur's Smile, The Human Animal in Early Greek Art* (Princeton, 2003).

Ceramics in Context Scheffer, C. (ed.), *Ceramics in context : proceedings of the Internordic Colloquium on Ancient Pottery held at Stockholm, 13–15 June 1997* (Stockholm, 2001).

Cesare, *Statue in Immagine* de Cesare, M., *Le statue in immagine, Studi sulle raffigurazioni di statue nella pittura vascolare greca* (Rome, 1997).

Christiansen and Melander, *Proceedings* Christiansen, J. and Melander, T., *Proceedings of the 3rd Symposium on Ancient Greek and Related Pottery, Copenhagen 31.8.–4.9.87* (Copenhagen, 1988).

Cité des Images *La Cité des Images, Religion et Société en Grèce Antique* (Lausanne, 1984).

Connor & Jackson, *Melbourne* Connor, P. and Jackson, H., *Greek Vases at The University of Melbourne* (Melbourne, 2000).

Cook, *Zeus* Cook, A., *Zeus* (Cambridge, 1914–40).

Corinth

Cristofani, *Etruschi* Cristofani, M., *Civilta degli Etruschi* (Milan, 1985).

Crouwel, *Chariots* Crouwel, J. H., *Chariots and other Wheeled Vehicles in Iron Age Greece, Allard Pierson Series* 9 (Amsterdam, 1992).

CV *Corpus Vasorum Antiquorum.*

Cygielmann, *Euphronios* Cygielmann, M., et al. (eds.), *Euphronios, Atti del Seminario Internazionale di Studi, Arezzo 27–28 Maggio 1990* (Florence, 1992).

Cygielman and Mangani Cygielman, M. and Mangani, E., *La Collezione Chigi-Zondadari, Museo Archeologico di Siena* (Rome, 1991).

Darracott, *Ricketts and Shannon* Darracott, J., *All for Art, The Ricketts and Shannon Collection* (1979).

Dasen, *Dwarfs* Dasen, V., *Dwarfs in Ancient Egypt and Greece* (Oxford, 1993).

DdA *Dialoghi di Archeologia* 10 (1992) 2.

Delavaud-Roux, *Danses Armées* Delavaud-Roux, M-H., *Les Danses Armées en Grèce Antique* (Aix-en-Provence, 1993).

Delavaud-Roux, *Danses Pacifiques* Delavaud-Roux, M-H., *Les danses pacifiques en Grèce antique* (Aix-en-Provence, 1994).

Delli Ponti, *Lecce* Delli Ponti, G., *Museo Provinciale, Lecce* (Rome, 1990).

Demakopoulou and Konsola Demakopoulou, K. and Konsola, D., *Archaeological Museum of Thebes* (Athens, 1981).

De Miro, *Templi* De Miro, E., *La Valle dei Templi* (Palermo, 1994).

Denoyelle, *Euphronios* Denoyelle, M. (ed.), *Euphronios, peintre à Athènes au VIe siècle avant J.-C.,[exposition], Musée du Louvre, Paris, 18 septembre–31 décembre 1990* (Paris, 1992).

De Puma and Penny Small, *Murlo* De Puma, R. D., and Penny Small, J. (eds.), *Murlo and the Etruscans, Art and Society in Ancient Etruria* (Madison, 1994).

Deppert, *Frankfurt*   Deppert, K., *Attische Vasen des 6. und 5. Jahrhunderts in Frankfurt* (1970).

DialHist   *Dialogues d'Histoire Ancienne* 28 (2002) 1.

Dörig & Gigon, *Titanen*   Dörig, J. & Gigon, O., *Der Kampf der Götter und Titanen* (Olten, 1961).

Dotzler, *Ornament*   Dotzler, G., *Ornament als Zeichen, Methodologische Probleme der archäologischen Interpretation, Arbeiten zur Urgeschichte* 8 (Frankfurt, 1984).

Drivaud, *Amiens*   Drivaud, S. *et al.*, *Les collections archéologiques du Musée de Picardie, Amiens* (Amiens, 1990).

Duby and Perrot, *Femmes*   Duby, G., and Perrot, M. (eds.), *Histoire des femmes* (Plon, 1991).

Ducrey, *Guerre*   Ducrey, P., *Guerre et Guerriers dans la Grèce Antique* (Paris, 1985).

Dugas, *Délos* X   Dugas, C., *Exploration archeologique de Délos*, X

Durand, *Sacrifice*   Durand, J.-L., *Sacrifice et Labour en Grèce ancienne* (Paris, 1986).

Ebertshäuser & Waltz   Ebertshäuser, H., and Waltz, M., *Vasen—Bronzen—Terrakotten des klassischen Altertums* (Munich, 1981).

Ephemeris   *Ephemeris Archaiologike* 140 (2000).

Expedition   *Expedition, Bulletin of the Museum of the University of Pennsylvania* 44 (2002).

Fantham, *Women*   Fantham, E., *et al.*, *Women in the Classical World, Image and Text* (New York, 1994).

Fellmann, *Polyphem-Abenteuer*   Fellmann, B., *Die antiken Darstellungen des Polyphem- Abenteuers* (Munich, 1978).

Fellmuth, *Jenaer Maler*   Fellmuth, N., *et al.*, *Der Jenaer Maler, Eine Töpferwerkstatt im klassischen Athen* (Wiesbaden, 1996).

Fest Bakalakis   *Kernos, timetike prosphora ston kathegete Georgio Bakalaki* (Thessaloniki, 1972).

Fest Brommer   Höckmann, U. and Krug, A. (eds.), *Festschrift für Frank Brommer* (Mainz, 1977).

Fest Hampe   Cahn, H. A. and Simon, E. (eds.), *Tainia, Festschrift für Roland Hampe* (Mainz, 1970).

Fest Himmelmann   Cain, H.-U., Gabelmann, H., and Salzmann, D. (eds.), *Festschrift für Nikolaus Himmelmann* (Bonn, 1989).

Fest Jale Inan   Basgelen, N. and Lugal, M. (eds.), *Festschrift für Jale Inan* (Istanbul, 1989).

Fest Lauffer   Kalcyk, H., et al. (eds.), *Studien zur Alten Geschichte, Festschrift Siegfried Lauffer* (Rome, 1986).

Fest Thimme   Metzler, D., Otto, B., and Müller-Wirth, C. (eds.), *Antidoron, Festschrift für Jürgen Thimme zum 65. Geburtstag am 26. September 1982* (Karlsruhe, 1983).

Firenze, Vasi Attici   Esposito, A. M., and Tommaso, G. (eds.), *Museo Archeologico Nazionale di Firenze, Vasi Attici* (Firenze, 1993).

Fisher & Wees   Fisher, N. und Wees, H. v. (eds.), *Archaic Greece: New Approaches and New Evidence* (Swansea, 1998).

Flaceliere and Devambez   Flaceliere, R., and Devambez, P., *Héracles, Images & Récits* (Paris, 1966).

Fournier-Christol, *Olpes* Fournier-Christol, C., *Catalogue des olpes attiques du Louvre de 550 à 480 environ* (Paris, 1990).
Frontisi-Ducroux, *Masque* Frontisi-Ducroux, F., *Du masque au visage, aspects de l'identité en Grèce ancienne* (Paris, 1995).
Frontisi-Ducroux and Vernant Frontisi-Ducroux, F. and Vernant, J-P., *Dans l'oeil du miroir* (Paris, 1997).

Galinsky, *Herakles Theme* Galinsky, G., *The Herakles Theme* (Oxford, 1972).
Garland, *Gods* Garland, R., *Introducing New Gods* (London, 1991).
Garland, *Deformity* Garland, R., *The Eye of the Beholder, Deformity and Disability in the Graeco-Roman World* (London, 1995).
Ghiron-Bistagne, *Recherches* Ghiron-Bistagne, P., *Recherches sur les Acteurs dans la Grèce Antique* (Paris, 1976).
Giudice, *Phanyllis* Giudice, F., *I Pittori della Classe di Phanyllis*, i, (Catania, 1983).
Goddess and Polis Neils, J., *et al.*, *Goddess and Polis, The Panathenaic Festival in Ancient Athens* (Princeton, 1992).
Gorbunova, *Chernofigurnie* Gorbunova, K., *Chernofigurnie atticheskie vazi v Ermitazhe, Katalog* (Leningrad, 1983).
Grabow, *Schlangenbilder* Grabow, E., *Schlangenbilder in der griechischen schwarzfigurigen Vasenkunst* (Paderborn, 1998).
Grassi and Bartoli, *Arezzo* Zamarchi Grassi, P. and Bartoli, D., *Museo archeologico nazionale G. Cilnio Mecenate, Arezzo* (Rome, 1993).
GRBS *Greek, Roman and Byzantine Studies* 42 (2001).
Greco and Pontrandolfo, *Fratte* Greco, G., and Pontrandolfo, A. (eds.), *Fratte, un insediamento etrusco-campano* (Modena, 1990).
Green and Handley, *Theatre* Green, R. and Handley, E., *Images of the Greek Theatre* (London, 1995).
Guazzelli, *Antesterie* Guazzelli, T, *Le Antesterie, Liturgie e pratiche simboliche* (Florence).
Guida Bologna Govi, C. and Vitali, D., (eds.), *Guida, Museo Civico Archeologico di Bologna* (Bologna, 1982).
Guides Lund, J., and Rasmussen, B. B., *Guides to the National Museum, The Collection of Near Eastern and Classical Antiquities* (Copenhagen, 1995).
GVGetty *Greek Vases in the J.Paul Getty Museum.*

Haffner, *Heiligtümer* Haffner, A. (ed.), *Heiligtümer und Opferkulte der Kelten* (Stuttgart, 1995).
Hadjidakis, *Delos* Hadjidakis, P. J., *Delos* (Athens, 2003).
Halm-Tisserant, *Cannibalisme* Halm-Tisserant, M., *Cannibalisme et immortalité, l'enfant dans le chaudron en Grèce ancienne* (Paris, 1993).
Halm-Tisserant, *Realités* Halm-Tisserant, V., *Réalités et imaginaire des supplices en Grèce ancienne* (Paris, 1998).
Hamdorf, *Dionysos* Hamdorf, D., *Dionysos, Bacchus, Kult und Wandlungen des Weingottes* (Munich, 1986).
Harrison, *Odyssey* Harrison, J., *Myths of the Odyssey* (London, 1982).
Hedreen, *Silens* Hedreen, G. M., *Silens in Attic Black-figure Vase-painting* (Michigan, 1992).

Heesen, *Theodor* Heesen, P., *The J. L. Theodor Collection of Attic Black-Figure Vases* (Amsterdam, 1996).

Heisserer, *Stovall Museum* Heisserer, A. (ed.), *Classical Antiquities, The Collection of the Stovall Museum of Science and History* (Oklahoma, 1986).

Herrmann, *Omphalos* Herrmann, H-V., *Omphalos* (Münster, 1959).

Holmberg, *Rycroft Painter* Holmberg, E. J., *On the Rycroft Painter and other Black-Figure Vase-Painters with a Feeling for Nature* (Jonsered, 1992).

Holmberg, *Red-Line Painter* Holmberg, E. J., *The Red-Line Painter and the Workshop of the Acheloos Painter* (Jonsered, 1990).

Hommes, Dieux et Héros *Hommes, Dieux et Heros de la Grèce*, Rouen, 23.10.1982–31.1.1983.

Hornbostel, *Kropatscheck* Hornbostel, W., *et al.*, *Aus Gräbern und Heiligtümern, Die Antikensammlung Walter Kropatscheck* (Mainz, 1980).

Hyatt, *Vase* Hyatt, S. (ed.), *The Greek Vase* (New York, 1981).

Immerwahr, *Attic Script* Immerwahr, H., *Attic Script, A Survey* (Oxford, 1990).

Janni, *Mare* Janni, P., *Il mare degli Antichi* (Bari, 1996).

Jb *Jahrbuch des Deutschen Archäologischen Instituts* 116 (2001).

JbRGZM *Jahrbuch des Römisch—Germanischen Zentralmuseums, Mainz* 45 (1998).

JHS *Journal of Hellenic Studies* 122 (2002).

Joffroy, *Vix* Joffroy, R., *Vix et ses Trésors* (Paris, 1979).

Jucker, *Antikensammlung* Jucker, I., *Aus der Antikensammlung des Bernischen Historischen Museums* (Bern, 1970).

Junker, *Mythos und Lebenswelt* Junker, K. (ed.), *Aus Mythos und Lebenswelt, Griechische Vasen aus der Sammlung der Universität Mainz* (Worms, 1999).

JWalt *Journal of the Walters Art Gallery* 59 (2001).

Kachler, *Theatermaske* Kachler, K. G., *Zur Entstehung und Entwicklung der griechischen Theatermaske* (Basel, 1991).

Kenner, *Verkehrte Welt* Kenner, H., *Das Phänomen der Verkehrten Welt* (Klagenfurt, 1970).

Kephalidou, *Nikitis* Kephalidou, E., *Nikitis, Eikonographiki meleti tou archaiou ellinikou athlitismou* (Thessaloniki, 1996).

Kerenyi, *Dionysos* Kerenyi, K., *Dionysos* (London, 1976).

Keuls, *Phallus* Keuls, E., *The Reign of the Phallus* (New York, 1985).

Knittlmayer, *Demokratie* Knittlmayer, B., *Die Attische Demokratie und ihre Helden, Darstellungen des trojanischen Sagenkreises im 6. und frühen 5. Jh.v.Chr.* (Heidelberg, 1997).

Kreuzer, *Frühe Zeichner* Kreuzer, B., *Frühe Zeichner 1500–500 vor Chr., Ägyptische, griechische und etruskische Vasenfragmente der Sammlung H. A. Cahn Basel* (Freiburg, 1992).

Krieger, *Peleus und Thetis* Krieger, X., *Der Kampf zwischen Peleus und Thetis* (Münster, 1975).

Kunst der Schale Vierneisel, K., and Kaeser, B. (eds.), *Kunst der Schale, Kultur des Trinkens* (Munich, 1990).

Kurtz, *AWL* Kurtz, D., *Athenian White Lekythoi* (Oxford, 1975).

Kurtz and Boardman, *Burial Customs* Kurtz, D. & Boardman, J., *Greek Burial Customs* (London, 1971).

Kurtz and Boardman, *Thanatos* Kurtz, D. C., and Boardman, J., *Thanatos, Tod und Jenseits bei den Griechen* (Mainz, 1985).

Lacroix, *Etudes* Lacroix, L., *Etudes d'archeologie numismatique* (Paris, 1974).
La musique Birchler Emery, P. et al., *La musique et la danse dans l'Antiquité, Regards sur les collections du Musée d'art et d'histoire de Geneve* (Geneva, 1996).
Lang, *Life, Death and Litigation* Lang, M., *Life, Death and Litigation in the Athenian Agora, American School of Classical Studies at Athens* 23 (Princeton, 1994).
Laser, *Sport und Spiel* Laser, S., *Sport und Spiel, Archeologia Homerica* (Göttingen, 1987).
Laufer, *Kaineus* Laufer, E., *Kaineus, Studien zur Ikonographie, RdA* Supp.1 (Rome, 1985).
Laurens, *Montpellier* Laurens, A., *Société Archéologique de Montpellier, Catalogue des Collections*, II (Montpellier, 1984).
Laurens and Pomian, Anticmanie Laurens, A-F. and Pomian, K., *L'Anticmanie, la collection d'antiquités aux 18e et 19e siècles* (Paris, 1992).
Lawler, *Dance* Lawler, L., *Dance in Ancient Greece* (London, 1964).
Lazarow, *Bulgaria* Lazarow, M., *Ancient Pottery from Bulgaria* (Sofia, 1990).
Lehnstaedt Lehnstaedt, K., *Prozessionsdarstellungen auf attischen Vasen* (1970).
LIMC *Lexicon Iconographicum Mythologiae Classicae.*
Lioutas, *Lekanai* Lioutas, A., *Attische schwarzfigurige Lekanai und Lekanides* (Würzburg, 1987).
Lippolis, *Eroi* Lippolis, E., *Gli eroi di Olimpia, lo sport nella societa Greca e Magnogreca* (Taranto, 1992).
Lissarrague, *Banquet* Lissarrague, F., *The Aesthetics of the Greek Banquet, Images of Wine and Ritual* (Princeton, 1990).
Lissarrague, *Céramique* Lissarrague, F. et al. (eds.), *Céramique et peinture Grecques, Modes d'emploi, Actes du colloque internat., Ecole du Louvre*, April 1995 (Paris, 1999).
Lissarrague, *Guerrier* Lissarrague, F., *L'Autre Guerrier, Archers, Peltastes, Cavaliers dans l'Imagerie Attique* (Paris-Rome, 1990).
Lissarrague, *Greek Vases* Lissarrague, F., *Greek vases, the Athenians and their images* (2001).
Lissarrague & Thelamon Lissarrague, F., Thelamon, F. (eds.), *Image et Céramique Grecque* (Rouen, 1983).
Lonis, *Guerre* Lonis, R., *Guerre et religion en Grèce à l'époque classique* (Paris, 1979).
Looking at Greek Vases Spivey, N. and Rasmussen, T. (eds.), *Looking at Greek Vases* (Cambridge, 1991).
Lund & Rasmussen Lund, J., and Rasmussen, B. B., *Guides to the National Museum, The Collection of Near Eastern and Classical Antiquities* (Copenhagen, 1995).
Luxusgeschirr *Luxusgeschirr keltischer Fürsten, Griechische Keramik nördlich der Alpen, Sonderausstellung des Mainfränkischen Museums Würzburg* (Würzburg, 1995).

Maas and Snyder, *Instruments* Maas, M. and Snyder, J. M, *Stringed Instruments of Ancient Greece* (New Haven, 1989).
Manakidou, *Parastaseis* Manakidou, E.P., *Parastaseis me Armata (8os-5os ai. p.Ch.). Paratiriseis stin Eikonographia tous* (Thessaloniki, 1994).
Mannack, *Einführung* Mannack, T., *Griechische Vasenmalerei, Eine Einführung* (Darmstadt, 2002).

Marquardt, *Pan* Marquardt, *Pan in der hellenistischen und kaiserzeitlichen Plastik* (Bonn, 1995).

May, *Jouer* May, R., *et al.*, *Jouer dans l'Antiquité, Musée d'Archeologie Méditerranéenne, Centre de la Vieille Charité* (Marseille, 1991).

Meddelelser *Meddelelser fra Ny Carlsberg Glyptotek* NS 4 (2002).

MededAPM *Mededelingenblad, Vereniging van Vrianden van het Allard PiersonMuseum* 78 (2000).

Meded Rome *Mededelingen van het Nederlands Instituut te Rome* 11 (1984).

Mertens, *White Ground* Mertens, J., *Attic White Ground, its development on shapes other than lekythoi* (New York, 1977).

MetMusJ *Metropolitan Museum Journal* 34 (1999).

Meyer, *Medeia* Meyer, H., *Medeia und die Peliaden* (Rome, 1980).

Mind and Body Tzachou-Alexandri, O., *Mind and Body, Athletic Contests in Ancient Greece* (Athens, 1988).

MiscGreca *Miscellanea Graeca.*

MiscManni *Miscellanea di Studi Classici in onore de Eugenio Manni* (Rome, 1979).

MittIran *Archäologische Mitteilungen aus Iran, N.F* 32 (2000).

MM *Kunstwerke der Antike, Munzen und Medaillen, A. G., Basel, sale catalogue.*

Modi e funzioni Gigante, M., *et al.*, *Modi e funzioni del racconto mitico nella ceramica Greca, Italiota ed Etrusca dal VI al IV secolo A.C.* (Salerno, 1995).

Mommsen, *Exekias* I Mommsen, H., *Exekias I, Die Grabtafeln* (Mainz, 1998).

Monumenti *Monumenti inediti pubblicati dall'Instituto di Corrispondenza Archeologica* (Rome, 1829–91).

Moon, *Iconography* Moon, W. (ed.), *Ancient Greek Art and Iconography* (Madison, 1983).

Moraw, *Mänade* Moraw, S., *Die Mänade in der attischen Vasenmalerei des 6. und 5. Jahrhunderts v.Chr.* (Mainz, 1998).

Moret, *Sphinx* Moret, J.-M., *Oedipe, la Sphinx et les Thébains* (Rome, 1984).

Musée Saint-Raymond *L'Art Grec au Musée Saint-Raymond, Catalogue raisonné d'une partie de la collection* (Toulose, n.d.).

Mythen, Mensen en Muziek *Mythen, Mensen en Muziek, een expositie over muziek in de oudheid, museum het valkhof nijmegen, Mededelingblad* 75–76 (Amsterdam, 1999).

Naked Truths Koloski-Ostrow, A. O., and Lyons, C. L., *Naked Truths, Women, Sexuality and Gender in Classical Art and Archaeology* (London, 1997).

Nicosia, *Itinerari* Nicosia, F., *Itinerari archeologici in Toscana* (Firenze, 1990).

Neils & Oakley, *Age* Neils, J. and Oakley, J., *Coming of Age, Images of Childhood from the Classical Past* (New Haven, 2003).

Neils, *Parthenon Frieze* Neils, J., *The Parthenon Frieze* (Cambridge, 2001).

Nick, *Parthenos* Nick, G., *Die Athena Parthenos, Studien zum griechischen Kultbild und seiner Rezeption, AM 19. Beiheft* (Mainz, 2002).

Nilsson, *Religion* Nilsson, M., *Geschichte der griechischen Religion* (Munich, 1941–50).

Oakley, *Achilles Painter* Oakley, J. H., *The Achilles Painter* (Mainz, 1997).

Oakley and Sinos, *Wedding* Oakley, J. H., and Sinos, R. H., *The wedding in ancient Athens* (Madison, 1993).

Oakley, *Gennadius* Oakley, J. H. (ed.), *Athenian Potters and Painters, Cat. of the Exhibit, December 1, 1994–March 1, 1995, Gennadius Lib. American School* (Athens, 1994).

Ohly, *Geleitwort* Ohly, D., *Geleitwort für den Besucher* (Munich, 1968).
OlForsch *Olympische Forschungen.*
Olmos, *Lagunillas* Olmos, R., *Vasos griegos, Colleccion Condes de Lagunillas* (Zurich, 1990).
Olmos, *Habana* Olmos, R., *Catalogo de los Vasos Griegos del Museo Nacional de Bellas Artes de La Habana* (Madrid, 1993).
Onians, *Classical Art* Onians, J., *Classical Art and the Cultures of Greece and Rome* (New Haven, 1999).
OpuscRom *Opuscula Romana, Edidit Institutum Romanum Regni Sueciae* **19 (1993)**.
Osborne, *Archaic and Classical* Osborne, R., *Archaic and Classical Greek Art, Oxford History of Art* (Oxford, 1998).
Oxford Companion Hornblower, S. and Spawforth, A. (eds.), *The Oxford Companion to Classical Civilization* (Oxford, 1998).

Pace, *Sicilia Antica* Pace, B., *Arte e Civilta delle Sicilia Antica*, 1ˢᵗ edn. (Milan,1938–49).
Pandora Reeder, E. D., *et al.*, *Pandora, Women in Classical Greece* (Baltimore, 1995).
Panvini, *Gelas* Panvini, R., *Gelas, Storia e archeologia dell'antica Gela* (Torino, 1996).
Panvini, *Museo* Panvini, R. (ed.), *Gela. Il Museo archeologico* (Gela, 1998).
Para Beazley, J. D., *Paralipomena* (Oxford, 1971).
Papers *Papers on the Amasis Painter and his World* (Malibu, 1987).
Parke, *Festivals* Parke, H., *Festivals of the Athenians* (London, 1977).
Paul, *Meisterwerke* Paul, E., *Universität Leipzig, Antikenmuseum, 50 Meisterwerke* (Leipzig,1994).
Paul, *Sponsoren* Paul, E. (ed.), *Sponsoren des Antikenmuseums gestern und heute* (Leipzig).
Pedley, *Art and Archaeology* Pedley, J. G., *Greek Art and Archaeology* (New Jersey, 1993).
Peifer, *Eidola* Peifer, E., *Eidola und andere mit dem Sterben verbundene Flügelwesen in der attischen Vasenmalerei in spätarchaischer und klassischer Zeit* (Frankfurt, 1989).
Pelling, *Tragedy* Pelling, C. (ed.), *Greek Tragedy and the Historian* (Oxford, 1997).
Petrakou, *Marathon* Petrakou, V. C., *Ho Marathon* (Athens, 1995).
Pfisterer-Haas, *Alte Frauen* Pfisterer-Haas, S., *Darstellungen alter Frauen in der griechischen Kunst* (Frankfurt, 1989).
Pickard-Cambridge Pickard-Cambridge, A., *The Dramatic Festivals of Athens* (Oxford, 1953).
Pickard-Cambridge2 Pickard-Cambridge, A., *The Dramatic Festivals of Athens*, 2ⁿᵈ edn. (Oxford, 1968).
Pickard-Cambridge, *Dithyramb* Pickard-Cambridge, A., *Dithyramb, Tragedy and Comedy* (Oxford, 1962).
Pochmarski, *Dionysische Gruppen* Pochmarski, E., *Dionysische Gruppen, eine typologische Untersuchung zur Geschichte des Stützmotivs* (1990).
Polacco, *Teatro di Siracusa* Polacco, L. (ed.), *Il teatro antico di Siracusa, pars altera* (Padua, 1990).
Poliakoff, *Combat Sports* Poliakoff, M. B., *Combat Sports in the Ancient World, Competition, Violence and Culture* (Yale, 1987).
Popovic, *Belgrade* Popovic, L. B., *National Museum of Belgrade, Collection of Greek Antiquities* (Belgrade, 1994).

Potters and Painters   Oakley, J. H., *et al., Athenian Potters and Painters, The Conference Proceedings* (Oxford, 1997).

Prag, *Oresteia*   Prag, A., *The Oresteia* (Warminster, 1985).

Proceedings   Docter, R. F. and Moormann, E. M. (eds.), *Proceedings of the 15th International Congress of Classical Archaeology, Amsterdam, July 12–17, 1998* (Amsterdam, 1999).

QuadTic   *Numismatica e Antichita Classiche, Quaderni Ticinesi.*

RA   *Revue Archeologique* (2000).

REA   *Revue des Études Anciennes* 25 (2001).

Rastrelli, *Chiusi*   Rastrelli, A., *Museo Archeologico di Chiusi* (Rome, 1991).

Rebecchi, *Spina*   Rebecchi, F. (ed.), *Spina e il delta Padano, Reflessioni sul catalogo e sulla mostra ferrarese* (Ferrara, 1998).

Recke, *Gewalt*   Recke, M., *Gewalt und Leid: Das Bild des Krieges bei den Athenern im 6. und 5. Jh. v. Chr.* (Istanbul, 2002).

Reinsberg, *Ehe*   Reinsberg, C., *Ehe, Hetärentum und Knabenliebe im antiken Griechenland* (Munich, 1989).

Richter & Milne   Richter, G. & Milne, M., *Shapes and Names of Athenian Vases* (New York, 1935).

Rivista   *Rivista di Archeologia.*

RivIst   *Rivista del R. Istituto di Archeologia e Storia d'Arte.*

Rizza, *Sicilia*   Rizza, G. (ed.), *I vasi attici ed altre ceramiche coeve in Sicilia, Atti del convegno internazionale* (Catania).

Rnjak, *Teatar*   Rnjak, D., *Anticki Teatar na tlu Jugoslavije, Antique Theater in the territory of Yugoslavia* (Novi Sad, 1979).

Robertson, *Vase-Painting*   Robertson, C. M., *The art of vase-painting in classical Athens* (Cambridge, 1992).

Romanelli, *Tarquinia*   Romanelli, P., *Tarquinia* (Rome, 1940).

Ronan, *Hekate*   Ronan, S. (ed.), *The Goddess Hekate, Studies in Ancient Pagan and Christian Religion & Philosophy* 1 (Hastings, 1992).

Rühfel, *Kind*   Rühfel, H., *Das Kind in der Griechischen Kunst* (Mainz, 1984).

Rumpf, *MuZ*   Rumpf, A., *Malerei und Zeichnung* (Munich, 1953).

Sakowski, *Dreifußkessel*   Sakowski, A., *Darstellungen von Dreifußkesseln in der griechischen Kunst bis zum Beginn der Klassischen Zeit* (Frankfurt, 1997).

Santi, *Collezioni*   Santi, M. F. (ed.), *Le collezioni di antichita nella cultura antiquaria Europea, RivIst* Supplement 21 (Rome, 1999).

Schauenburg, *Helios*   Schauenburg, K., *Helios* (Berlin, 1955).

Schefold and Jung, *Argonauten*   Schefold, K., Jung, F., *Die Sagen von den Argonauten, von Theben und Troia in der klassischen und hellenistischen Kunst* (Munich, 1989).

Schefold and Jung, *Urkönige*   Schefold, K., and Jung, F., *Die Urkönige, Perseus, Bellerophon, Herakles und Theseus in der klassischen und hellenistischen Kunst* (Munich, 1988).

Schefold, *Göttersage*   Schefold, K., *Die Göttersage in der klassischen und hellenistischen Kunst* (Munich, 1981).

Schefold, *Heldensagen*   Schefold, K., *Götter und Heldensagen der Griechen in der spätarchaischen Kunst* (Munich, 1978).

Schefold, *Heroes*   Schefold, K., *Gods and Heroes in Late Archaic Greek Art* (translation, Cambridge, 1992).

Schefold, *Hocharchaische Kunst*   Schefold, K., *Götter- und Heldensagen der Griechen in der Früh- und Hocharchaischen Kunst* (Munich, 1993)

Scheibler, *Malerei*   Scheibler, I., *Griechische Malerei der Antike* (Munich, 1994).

Scheibler, *Töpferkunst*   Scheibler, I., *Griechische Töpferkunst, Herstellung, Handel und Gebrauch der antiken Tongefäße* (Munich, 1983).

Scheibler, *Töpferkunst2*   Scheibler, I., *Griechische Töpferkunst, Herstellung, Handel und Gebrauch der antiken Tongefäße*, 2nd edn. (Munich, 1995).

Schiffler, *Typologie des Kentauren*   Schiffler, B., *Die Typologie des Kentauren in der antiken Kunst* (Frankfurt, 1976).

Schmitt Pantel, *Banquet*   Schmitt Pantel, P., *La cité au banquet, histoire des repas publics dans les cités grecques* (Rome, 1992).

Schnapp, *Chasseur*   Schnapp, A., *Le chasseur et la cité, Chasse et érotique dans la Grèce ancienne* (Paris, 1997).

Schöne, *Thiasos*   Schöne, A., *Der Thiasos, Eine ikonographische Untersuchung über das Gefolge des Dionysos in der attischen Vasenmalerei des 6.u.5. Jhs.v.Chr.* (Göteborg, 1987).

Schwarz, Washington   Schwarz, S. J., *Greek Vases In the National Museum of Natural History Smithsonian Institution Washington, D.C.* (Rome, 1996).

Semeraro, *Salento arcaico*   Semeraro, G., *En niysi, Ceramica greca e societa nel Salento arcaico* (Bari, 1997).

SES   *Senri Ethnological Studies.*

Settis, *Greci*   Settis, S. (ed.), *I Greci, Storia Cultura Arte Societa 2, Una storia greca, 1.Formazione* (Turin, 1996).

Shapiro, *Myth into Art*   Shapiro H. A., *Myth into Art, Poet and Painter in Classical Athens* (London, 1994).

Shapiro, *Personifications*   Shapiro, H. A., *Personifications in Greek Art, The Representation of Abstract Concepts 600–400 BC* (Zurich, 1993).

Shapiro, *San Antonio*   Shapiro, H. A., *et al.* (eds.), *Greek Vases in the San Antonio Museum of Art* (San Antonio, 1995).

Shapiro, *Southern Collections*   Shapiro, H. (ed.), *Art, Myth and Culture, Greek Vases from Southern Collections* (Tulane, 1981).

Shapiro, *Tyrants*   Shapiro, H. A., *Art and Culture under the Tyrants in Athens* (Mainz, 1989).

Sicilia greca   *La Sicilia greca, det grecisca Sicilien, mostra organizzata della regione Siciliana* (Palermo, 1989).

Sidorova, *Pushkin Museum*   Sidorova, N. A., *et al.*, *Antique Painted Pottery in the Pushkin State Museum of Fine Art, Moscow* (Moscow, 1985).

Simon, *Götter*   Simon, E., *Die Götter der Griechen* (Munich, 1969).

Simon, *Festivals*   Simon, E., *Festivals of Attica, an Archaeological Commentary* (Wisconsin, 1983).

Simon & Hirmer   Simon, E. & Hirmer, M., *Die Griechischen Vasen* (Munich, 1976).

Simon, *Ausgewählte Schriften*   Simon, E., *Ausgewählte Schriften*, I, *Griechische Kunst* (Mainz, 1998).

Snowden, *Blacks*   Snowden, F., *Blacks in Antiquity* (Cambridge, Mass., 1970).

Solon to Salamis   Athens *Comes of Age, from Solon to Salamis* (Princeton, 1978).

SothPB   *Sotheby-Parke-Bernet, New York, sale catalogue.*

Sparkes, *Red and Black* Sparkes, B. A., *The Red and the Black* (London, 1996).

Stackelberg Stackelberg, O., *Die Gräber der Hellenen* (Berlin, 1937).

Stähler, *Patroklos* Stähler, K., *Grab und Psyche des Patroklos* (M_nster, 1967).

Steinhart, *Auge* Steinhart, M., *Das Motiv des Auges in der griechischen Bildkunst* (Mainz, 1995).

Stern, *Labours* Stern, F., *The Labours of Herakles on Antiquities from West Coast Collections* (1976).

Stips Votiva Gnade, M. (ed.), *Stips Votiva, Papers presented to C. M. Stibbe* (Amsterdam, 1991).

StudAnt *Universita di Lecce, Studi di Antichita.*

Studies Oswald D-E; Rosen, R. M. and Farrell, J. (eds.), *Nomodeiktes, Studies in Honor of Martin Oswald* (Michigan, 1993).

Studi Nenci Alessandri, S. (ed.), *Historie, Studi offerti dagli allievi a Giuseppe Nenci in occasione del suo settantesimo compleanno* (1994).

Sweet, *Sport* Sweet, W. E., *Sport and Recreation in Ancient Greece, A Source Book with Translations* (Oxford, 1987).

Ta Attika Panvini, R. and Giudice, F. (eds.), Ta *Attika, Attic Figured Vases from Gela* (Rome, 2003)

***Taranto* I.2** Alessio, A., *et al.*, *Catalogo del Museo Nazionale Archeologico di Taranto* I.2 (Taranto, 1990).

***Taranto* I.3** D'Amicis, A., *et al.*, *Catalogo del Museo Nazionale Archeologico di Taranto* I.3, *Atleti e Guerrieri, Tradizioni aristocratiche* (Taranto, ca. 1994).

***Taranto* 3.1** Lippolis, E. (ed.), *Catalogo. del Museo Archeologico di Taranto*, 3.1, *Taranto, la necropoli, aspetti e problemi della documentazione archeologica* (Taranto, 1990).

Thöne, *Nike* Thöne, C., *Ikonographische Studien zu Nike im 5.Jh.v.Chr., Untersuchungen zu Wirkungsweise und Wesensart, Archäologie & Geschichte* 8 (Heidelberg, 1999).

Tiverios, *Techni* Tiverios, M. A., *Elliniki techni, archaia angaia* (Athens, 1996).

Touchefeu-Meynier, *Thèmes Odysséens* Touchefeu-Meynier, O., *Thèmes Odysséens dans l'art antique* (Paris, 1968).

Trendall & Webster Trendall, A. & Webster, T., *Illustrations of Greek Drama* (London, 1971).

Trias de Arribas Trias de Arribas, G., *Ceramicas Griegas de la Peninsula Iberica* (Valencia, 1967– 68).

TrudyErm *Trudy Gosudarstvennogo Ermitazha.*

Tzachou-Alexandri, *Mind and Body* Tzachou-Alexandri, O., *Mind and Body, Athletic Contests in Ancient Greece* (Athens, 1988).

Uhlenbrock, *Herakles*, Uhlenbrock, J. P., *Herakles, passage of the hero through 1000 years of classical art* (New York, 1986).

Valavanis and Kourkoumelis, *Chaire* Valavanis, P., and Kourkoumelis, D., *Chaire kai piei, drinking vessels* (1996).

Vanhove, *deporte* Vanhove, D. (ed.), *El deporte en la Grecia antigua, la genesis del olimpismo, May 10–August 9, 1992* (Barcelona, 1992).

Vanhove, *Sport* Vanhove, D. (ed.), *Le Sport dans la Grèce Antique, du Jeu à la Competition, 23 Janvier–19 Avril 1992* (Gent, 1992).

van Straten, *Hiera Kala* van Straten, F. T., *Hiera Kala, Images of Animal Sacrifice in Archaic and Classical Greece* (Leiden, 1995).

Vases a Mémoire   Landes, C., and Laurens, A-F. *et al.* (eds.), *Les vases à mémoire, les collections de céramique Greque dans le midi de la France* (Montpellier, 1988).
Veder Greco   Braccesi, L., *et al.*, *Veder Greco, le necropoli di Agrigento, mostra internazionale, Agrigento, 2. maggio–31. luglio 1988* (Rome, 1988).
Verbanck-Pierard, *Hippocrate*   Verbanck-Pierard, A. (ed.), *Au Temps d'Hippocrate, Medecine et Societe en Grèce Antique* (Mariemont, 1998).
Vermeule, *Aspects*   Vermeule, E., *Aspects of Death in Early Greek Art and Poetry* (Berkeley, 1979).
Vickers, *Pottery*   Vickers, M., *Ancient Greek Pottery* (Oxford, 1999).
Vickers, *Vases*   Vickers, M., *Greek Vases* (Oxford, 1978).
Vidale, *Lavoro*   Vidale, M., *L'idea di un lavoro lieve. Il lavoro artigianale nelle immagini della ceramica greca fra il VI e il IV secolo a.c.* (Padua, 2002).
Vogt, *Griechische Literatur*   Vogt, E., *Griechische Literatur, Neues Handbuch der Literaturwissenschaft 2* (Wiesbaden, 1981).
Vojatzi, *Argonautenbilder*   Vojatzi, M., *Frühe Argonautenbilder* (Würzburg, 1982).

Weber, *Badekultur*   Weber, M., *Antike Badekultur* (Munich, 1996).
Wescoat, *Syracuse*   Wescoat, B. D. (ed.), *Syracuse, The Fairest Greek City, Ancient Art from the Museo Archeologico Regionale Paolo Orsi* (Atlanta, 1989).
Wijer, *Polyphemusavontuur*   Wijer, B. van de, *Iconologisch Onderzoek van het Polyphemusavontuur* (Leuven, 1982).
Williams, *Johns Hopkins*   Williams, E., *The Archaeological Collection of the Johns Hopkins University* (Baltimore, 1984).
Wolf, *Herakles*   Wolf, S. R., *Herakles beim Gelage, eine motiv- und bedeutungsgeschichtliche Untersuchung des Bildes in der archaisch- frühklassischen Vasenmalerei* (Köln, 1993).

Yegul, *Baths*   Yegul, F. K., *Baths and bathing in classical antiquity* (London, 1992).

Zimmermann, *Griechische Vasen*   Zimmermann, K., *Griechische Vasen des 7. bis 4. Jahrhunderts* (Frankfurt, 1973).
Ziomecki   Ziomecki, J., *Les représentations d'artisans sur les vases attiques* (Wroclaw, 1975).

Abbreviations of Decorated Areas

(A)	Obverse
(AH)	At handle
(B)	Reverse
(EX)	Exergue
(I)	Inside
(IZ)	Inside, zone around
(LD)	Lid
(N)	Neck
(OV)	Obverse (of a plate or plaque)
(PR)	Predella
(R)	Rim
(S)	Shoulder
(ST)	Stand
(UH)	Under handle

I. THE 'DEIANEIRA' SHAPE

1, pl. 1.1 LONDON, 1931.8–10.1. *ABV* 11.17; *Para* 8; *BAdd* 3.

1, note 4 TARANTO, 6504. *ABV* 10.2.

1, note 4 BERLIN, Univ. *ABV* 10.3

1, note 4 BUFFALO, G 600. *ABV* 12.22; *BAdd* 3; *Para* 8.

1, note 4 PARIS, CA 823. *ABV* 13.23; *BAdd* 3.

2, note 4 BRUSSELS, A 1368. *ABV* 12.24; *BAdd* 4; Schnapp, *Chasseur* 262, no.214 (parts).

2, note 1 BERLIN, F 1659. *ABV* 20.1; *BAdd* 6; *Ausgestellte Werke,* 66, no. 4 (part).

2, pl. 2.3 BONN, 602. *Para* 198.

3 ATHENS, 1055 (CC 669). *ABV* 347; *BAdd* 94.

II. THE 'SHOULDER-LEKYTHOS'

7–9, 55, 63, pl. 2.1A–C ATHENS, 413 (CC 677). *ABV* 75; *BAdd* 20; *LIMC*, VI, pl. 554, Nessos 120 (S); *RA* (1993) 244, fig. 8 (part); Schefold, *Heroes*, figs. 33–34; Shapiro, *Tyrants*, pl. 25B–C.

9 ATHENS, Acr., 295. *ARV²* 374.52; *BAdd* 226.

10, 19, 31 note 1, pl. 2.2 PARIS, CabMed, 277 (once Paris, Duke of Luynes 690). *CV*, I, pl. 46.1–2, 5–6; *Cité des Images,* 153, fig. 216 (BD).

12, pl. 4.1 ATHENS, Ceramicus, 6159. *ABV* 58.127; *BAdd* 16; Schnapp, *Chasseur,* 248, no.177 (drawing); Settis, *Greci*, 823, fig. 36.

13, pl. 3.3 PALERMO, 1855. *Sicilia greca*, 204, no.135 (part).

15 SYRACUSE, 21894. *Para* 201; *BAdd* 115; *DialHist*, 10 (1984) 216, fig. 10; Ahlberg-Cornell, *Myth,* 307, fig. 82 (drawing of BD); *Ta Attika*, 253.C19 (part); Schefold, *Hocharchaische Kunst,* 334, fig. 380 (part).

16 PARIS, Market. *ABV* 458.

16 ATHENS, Acr., 799. *ABV* 122.2, 116.19.

17 ATHENS, 1394. *ABV* 457.13.

17.1 WÜRZBURG, L 360. *ABV* 459.1 (Fat-Runner Group, Group of Vatican 52).

17.2 ROME, M 557. *ABV* 459.2 (Fat-Runner Group, Group of Vatican 52).

17.3 ROME, 24997. *ABV* 459.3 (Fat-Runner Group, Group of Vatican 52).

17.4 ATHENS, 9699 (N 939.1). *ABV* 459.4 (Fat-Runner Group, Group of Vatican 52).

17.5 ATHENS, 9700 (N 939.2). *ABV* 459.5 (Fat-Runner Group, Group of Vatican 52).

17.6 ATHENS, 9704 (N 939.3). *ABV* 459.6 (Fat-Runner Group, Group of Vatican 52).

17.9 ST. PETERSBURG, OL 12582. *ABV* 460.13; *Para* 201 (Fat-Runner Group, Group of Vatican 52).

17.10 LEIDEN, RO III.23. Bastet, *Rottiers*, pl. 30.415; *CV* I, pl. 17.1–2.

17.11 SYRACUSE, 44099. *ABV* 599.43; *BAdd* 141; Wescoat, *Syracuse*, 70, 113, no. 37 (A, B, colour pl. of A).

17.12 PARIS, CA 1265. *ABV* 460.1 (Near the Fat-Runner Group, Group of Vatican 52).

17.1 BELGRADE, 213. *ABV* 461.21 (Group of Vatican G 52); *JbRGZM*, 33 (1986) 1, 13, fig. 10.3 (drawing of part); Popovic, *Belgrade*, 245, no. 379 (part).

17.2 BRUSSELS, A 2128. *ABV* 461.28 (Group of Vatican G 52).

17.3 BOLOGNA, 85. *ABV* 461.27 (Group of Vatican G 52).

17.4 WÜRZBURG, 363. *ABV* 461.15 (Group of Vatican G 52).

17.1 ROME, 1394. *ABV* 470.92 (Cock Group).

17.2 CATANIA, 4124 (once Museo Biscari, 661). *ABV* 463.4 (Related to the Group of Vatican G 52); Barresi and Valastro, 34, no.13 (colour of parts).

17, note 1 TARQUINIA, RC 4194. *Archeo* 80 (1991) 71–72 (colour of A, I and IZ); *ADelt*, 41 (1986) 2, pl. 83B (I); Ahlberg-Cornell, *Herakles*, 115, no. IV 3 (I); Arias & Hirmer, pls. 49, XIV (colour of I, A, B); Barringer, *Divine Escorts*, pl. 104 (I); *CV* 2, pl. 21.5–6 (I, A); Dotzler, *Ornament*, pl. 9, fig. 39 (I); *LIMC*, VI, pl. 490, Nereides 264 (I, IZ); Laser, *Sport und Spiel*, 31, fig. 4 (drawing of part of A); Lawler, *Dance*, frontispiece (drawing of I); Rnjak, *Theater*, fig. 13 at p. 178 (I); Romanelli, *Tarquinia*, 115–116, figs. 65–66 (I, A); Schefold, *Heldensagen*, 129, fig. 165; Schefold, *Heroes*, fig. 165; Simon & Hirmer, pl. XXI (colour of I); Sonnabend, *Mensch*, 540, fig. 91 (I); Tiverios, *Techni*, 76–77, figs. 35–36 (colour of I and part of A).

18.4 BRUSSELS, R 333. *ABV* 460.2 (Group of Vatican G 52, Near the Fat-Runner Group).

18.5 BARCELONA, 412 (54). Vanhove, *deporte*, 306, no. 172; Trias de Arribas, pl. 23; Vanhove, *Sport*, 306, no. 172 (colour of part).

18 VATICAN, M 467. *ABV* 126.57 (Painter of Louvre F 6).

18 RHODES, 10645. *ABV* 156.52 (Painter of Louvre F 6).

18 SYRACUSE. *ABV* 126.43 (Painter of Louvre F 6).

18, pl. 6.1A–C LONDON, 1873.8–20.299 (B 548). *ABV* 154.58; *BAdd* 45; Angiolillo, *Pisistrato,* 150, figs. 85A–B (BD); *Annali,* 14 (1992) pl. 19.1 (part).

18, 21–22, pl. 7.1A–B ATHENS, 493 (CC 693). *ABV* 251.1; *Para* 112; *LIMC,* VIII, pl. 648, Persephone 169 (part of BD).

19 PARIS, CA 1340. *ABV* 458.

19 ATHENS, 397 (CC 895). *ABV* 505; *BAdd* 126.

19 ATHENS, 1056. *ABV* 70.4.

19, pls. 5.2, 6.2 (S, BD) OXFORD, 1934.353. *ABV* 70.8. *Para* 28.

20.2, pls. 15.4a–c PALERMO, 1894 (1896.2). *ABV* 385.30; *LIMC,* pl. 75, Herakles 2319.

22, pl. 7.5 PARIS, CA 178. *ABV* 249.16; *Para* 112; *LIMC,* VI, pl. 564, Nike 72 (part).

III. SUB-DEIANEIRA LEKYTHOI

26 BERLIN, F 1741. *Anz,* 1976, 217, fig. 5; *Jb,* 102 (1987) 47, fig. 30A (drawing).

26 LONDON, B 53. *ABV* 457.

26 ST. PETERSBURG, 1440 (ST 91). *ABV* 457.

27 WÜRZBURG, HA 446 (L 356). *ABV* 455; *BAdd* 114; *LIMC,* III, pl. 344, Dionysos 404; Schöne, *Thiasos,* pl. 18.1.

27 ATHENS, 497 (CC 676). *LIMC,* VII, 975, Kyknos I 62 (drawing); Schefold, *Heldensagen,* 202, fig. 202 (drawing).

28 PARIS, G 490 (EL 490). Schnapp, *Chasseur* 253, no.190 (BD).

28 NEW YORK, 41.162.36 (once New York, Gallatin). *ABV* 458; *CV* Gallatin, pl. 2.1.

29 GELA, MUNICIPIO. *Ta Attika,* 250.C7 (drawing of part); Vidale, *Lavoro,* 173–175, fig. 21 (drawing of part); Ziomecki, 28, 152.23.

30 ATHENS, 404 (CC 674). *ABV* 155.62, 688; *Para* 64; *BAdd* 45.

31, 37, pls. 11.3A–B, 12.4 ATHENS, 414 (CC 694). *ABV* 177.

IV. THE SHOULDER-LEKYTHOS OF ABOUT 540 TO 530

34 ATHENS, 379 (CC 705). *ABV* 61.1.

34 ATHENS, 1094 (CC 703). *ABV* 61.2.

34.3 ROME, 50653 (M 556). *ABV* 175.11 (Taleides Painter).

34.4 SAN SIMEON, 9955 (once Paris, market). *ABV* 453.3, 698 (Painter of the Nicosia Olpe [Smith]); *Para* 196; *BAdd* 114.

34.5 NAPLES, 81202 (H 2727). *ABV* 453.4 (Painter of the Nicosia Olpe [Smith]); *Para* 196.

34–35, pls. 10.1A–B, 12.1 ATHENS, 415 (CC 711). *ABV* 70.

35, 63, 67, pls. 10.2, 12.2 ATHENS, 371. *Para* 207.

35, 67 ATHENS, 576 (CC 698). *ABV* 70.

35, 36, pl. 12.5A–C ATHENS, 941 (9693). *LIMC*, VII, pl. 690, Kymnos I.25 (part).

36 COPENHAGEN, 6585. *ABV* 115.5 (Manner of Lydos).

36 ROME, 1226. *ABV* 201.2 (Charter House Painter).

36 RHODES, 11941. *Para* 80.1, 86.1 (FP Class, Group of Rhodes 11941).

37 ATHENS, 507 (CC 671). *ABV* 112.56 (Lydos); *Para* 44; *BAdd* 31; *Classical Antiquity*, 12 (1993) fig. 3 at 219 (I); Knittlmayer, *Demokratie*, pl. 9.3; *LIMC*, I, Achilleus 187; Lissarrague, *Guerrier*, 44, fig. 13 (drawing of I); *Mind and Body*, 150, no.38.

38 SYDNEY, 48.284 (once Borden Wood, Mrs. Winifred Lamb). *ABV* 175.13; *Para* 73; *BAdd* 49.

39, pl. 13.2 (part) ATHENS, 524 (CC 726). Ahlberg-Cornell, *Herakles*, 132, no. VII 2; *LIMC*, VIII, pl. 42, Triton 5B (part).

V. THE BEGINNING OF THE RED-FIGURE PERIOD

41, note 2 BOSTON, 89.273. *ABV* 144.4; *Para* 59; *BAdd* 39; *Potters and Painters*, 158, figs. 1–2 (A, B); *Hephaistos*, 9 (1988) 145, fig. 2 (SB).

41, note 2 LONDON, 1836.2–24.127 (B 210). *ABV* 144.7, 672.2, 686; *Para* 60; *BAdd* 39; *AntClass*, 58 (1989) pl. 2, fig. 3 (B); *Archeo*, 80 (October 1991) 77 (colour of A); Laurens and Pomian, *Anticmanie*, 274, fig. 3 (A); Blok, *Early Amazons*, pl. 3 (A); Boardman, *Greek Art*, 105, fig. 93 (colour of A); Brinkmann, *Beobachtungen*, 93, fig. D (drawing of part of A); Buitron-Oliver, *New Perspectives*, 130, fig. 9 (B); *BABesch*, 67 (1992) 69, fig. 8 (B); Carpenter, *Art and Myth*, fig. 321 (A); Lissarrague, *Céramique*, 180, fig. 5 (B); Christiansen and Melander, *Proceedings*, 432, figs. 10–11 (A, B); *Altertum*, 35 (1989) 2, 70, fig. 2 (A); *Fest Jale Inan*, 160, fig. 4 (part of A); *Hephaistos*, 11/12 (1992/93) 14, fig. 3 (part of A); *LIMC*, VIII, pl. 610, Oinopion 3 (B); Osborne, *Archaic and Classical*, 87, 105, fig. 50 (colour and colour of part of A); Pedley, *Art and Archaeology*, 188, fig. 6.67 (colour of A); *QuadTic*, 28 (1999) 124, pl. 1 (part of A); Schefold,

Heroes, figs. 13, 320; Shapiro, *Tyrants*, pl. 41C (B); Sparkes, *Red and Black*, 13, fig. I.6 (A); Tiverios, *Techni*, 84–85, figs. 45–46 (colour of A and part of A).

41, note 2 LONDON, 1849.5–18.10 (B 209). *ABV* 144.8, 686; *Para* 60; *BAdd* 39; Angiolillo, *Pisistrato*, 153, fig. 86 (B); Berard, *Image*, 11, figs. 5–6 (A, B); Boardman, *Greeks Overseas*, 153, fig. 194 (part).

41, note 2 LONDON, 1843.11–3.77 (B 333). *ABV* 676, 677, 678; Immerwahr, *Attic Script*, pl. 22.92 (BD); *Jb*, 101 (1986) 67, fig. 5 (drawing of part); *Papers*, 73, fig. 14 (part).

42 PALERMO, 471. *ABV* 454; *LIMC*, IV, pl. 122, Gigantes 143 (part).

42, pl. 14.3 NEW YORK, 07.286.43. *ABV* 454.2.

42, pl. 15.3 (part) MUNICH, 1892 (J 769). *ABV* 385.32; *BAdd* 102; *RivIst*, 6 (1954) 200 right; *Veder Greco*, 104, no. 6.

43, 44, 46, 52, 99, pl. 20.1 (S) DELOS, B 6.129 (547). *ABV* 379.274. *Para* 163, 168; *LIMC*, V, pl. 85, Herakles 2470 (part).

43 OXFORD, 1889.1012 (V 245). *ABV* 498; *Para* 212.1; *Ta Attika*, 273.D74 (parts).

44, pl. 14.2. PALERMO, GE 1896.1 (1851). *ABV* 379.276; *LIMC*, VII, pl. 708, Kyknos I 126 (part).

47 AREZZO, 1465. *AJA*, 99 (1995) 432, fig. 6 (A); *ARV²* 15.6, 1619; *Antike Welt*, 22 (1991) 2, 136, fig. 2 (part of A); *BAdd* 152; Nicosia, *Itinerari*, 9–10 (A, B); *Burlington Magazine*, 132 (December 1990) 893, fig. 91 (A); Cesare, *Statue in Immagine*, 57, fig. 9 (A); Cristofani, *Etruschi*, 56, figs. 20–21 (A, B); Denoyelle, *Euphronios*, 77, fig. 16 (A); Grassi and Bartoli, *Arezzo*, 30, 32, figs. 14A–B (colour of parts of A and B); *LIMC*, VII, pl. 588, Telamon 6 (part of A); *Para* 322; Cygielmann, *Euphronios*, pls. 1–21, 33, 40, 46–47.

49, pl. 15.1 VIENNA, 75. *ABV* 379.270 (Leagros Group); *BAdd* 100; *LIMC*, IV, pl. 539, Herakles 1443 (part); Bernhard-Walcher, *Antikes Leben*, 126, no.68 (part).

49 OXFORD, 1889.1010 (V 249). Brommer, *Herakles II*, 29, fig. 9 (drawing); *LIMC*, VI, pl. 18, Kerkopes 19 (part); Rizza, *Sicilia*, I, 184, fig. 3 (part); *Ta Attika*, 258.D10bis (part).

49 SYRACUSE, 20541. *Para* 213.1; *LIMC*, VI, pl.135, Leto 53 (drawing).

49 SYRACUSE, 20538. *Ta Attika*, 258.D10 (parts).

49 SYRACUSE, 20539. *Para* 213.2; *Ta Attika*, 278.F2 (parts).

49 SYRACUSE, 21149. *Para* 213; *BAdd* 118; *Ta Attika*, 278.F3 (parts).

50 PALERMO, 2212. Sakowski, *Dreifußkessel*, 402–403, figs. 45–47.

50 PALERMO, 1865 (2635). Brommer, *Herakles II*, 30, fig. 11 (drawing); Dasen, *Dwarfs*, pl. 71.2 (part).

50 MUNICH, 1893 (J. 773). *Veder Greco*, 103, no. 5.

50 NAPLES, 81191 (H 2430). *ABV* 380.286, 700 (Leagros Group).

50 OXFORD, 1929.463. *ABV* 380.285; *Para* 163.

50 ATHENS, 12482 (N 934). *ABV* 379.280.

50 ATHENS, 429 (CC 939). *ABV* 379.281.

50 DELOS, B 6137.546 (546). *ABV* 378.257; *Para* 163; *BAdd* 100.

50 CAMBRIDGE, GR 2.1955 (once Borden Wood, Mrs. Winifred Lamb). *ABV* 378.259; *BAdd* 100.

51 NAPLES, 81201 (H 2746). *ABV* 378.258; *Para* 163; *BAdd* 100; Brinkmann, *Beobachtungen*, 84, fig. B (drawing of part).

53 VIENNA, 364. *REA*, 90 (1988) 1–2, 57, fig. 7A–B.

53, pl. 16.3 NEW YORK, 06.1021.81. *ABV* 378.263; *LIMC*, VI, pl. 404, Mousa, Mousai 128 (part).

54 NEW YORK, 56.171.33 (once Deepdene, Hope). Brommer, *Herakles II*, 110, fig. 53 (drawing); Buitron-Oliver, *New Perspectives*, 46, figs. 12–13 (parts); *BullMetMus*, 15 (1956–57) 172, above; *Fest Himmelmann*, pl. 33.4–5; *MiscGraeca*, 7 (1985) pl. 3 (drawing); Pace, *Sicilia Antica*, 3, 323, fig. 63 (drawing).

54 LOST (once BERLIN, F 1960). *AK*, 18 (1975) 76, fig. 1(drawing); *Anz*, 1988, 45, fig. 5 (drawing); Brommer, *Odysseus*, 71, fig. 29 (drawing); *JWalt*, 4 (1941) 121, fig. 4 (drawing).

54 LONDON, B 554. *ABV* 379.268.

54 PARIS, MusRodin, 241 (946). *ABV* 378.254; *BAdd* 100.

54 TARANTO, 4417 (45). *Taranto* I.3, 305, no. 82.1 (part).

55, 109, pl. 16.2 (part) ATHENS, 1122 (CC 738). *ABV* 379.265.

55 NEW YORK, 06.1021.60. *ABV* 345.1.

55, 61, pls. 16.1A–B, 20.3 VIENNA, 753. Kurtz, *AWL*, pl. 4.2; *LIMC*, V, pl. 131, Herakles 3012; Sakowski, *Dreifußkessel*, 383–384, figs. 26–27 (BD).

VI. EARLY GROUPS OF CYLINDER SHAPED LEKYTHOI

59 AMSTERDAM, 2100. *ABV* 368.102, 389; *Para* 170.4; *BAdd* 98.

59 CHIUSI, 1812. *ABV* 368.97, 389; *Para* 162, 170; *BAdd* 98; Rastrelli, *Chiusi*, pl. 10 (colour of B).

59 ORVIETO, 2701 (186). *ABV* 368.98, 389; *Para* 170.2; *BAdd* 98.

60 ATHENS, Acr., 15124 (2560). *ABV* 337.32; *BAdd* 92; Holmberg, *Rycroft Painter,* 40, fig. 28; *HASB,* 17 (2000) pls. 3–4 (including drawing).

60 WÜRZBURG, 366. *ABV* 337.31 (Rycroft Painter); *LIMC*, V, pl. 130, Herakles 3000 (part).

61 MUNICH, 1885 (J 755). *Annali*, NS 2 (1995) 121, fig. 10 (part); Fellmann, *Polyphem-Abenteuer*, 125, pl. 20; Harrison, *Odyssey*, pl. 5 (drawing); *Kunst der Schale*, 137, fig. 19.8 (part); Ohly, *Geleitwort*, pl. 19 (part); Pace, *Sicilia Antica*, 3, 45, fig. 8 (drawing of part); *Pantheon*, 40 (1982) 213, fig. 3; Touchefeu-Meynier, *Thèmes Odysséens*, pl. 8.2; *Veder Greco*, 105, no. 7 (part); *Archeo*, 99 (MAY 1993) 47 left (colour of part).

63 SYRACUSE, 21127. Giudice, *Phanyllis*, I, pls.29.1, 6–7, 33.10; *Ta Attika*, 262.D24 (parts).

65, note 1 PARIS, S 1261 (F 194). Giudice, *Phanyllis*, 106, fig. 10 (drawing).

66, pl. 19.5 PALERMO, 2141 (V 996). *AntClass*, 3 (1934), 461, fig. 1 (drawing); Carpenter, *Art and Myth* fig. 127 (part); Felten, *Unterweltsdarstellungen*, fig. 11 (part); Giudice, *Phanyllis*, pl. 14.12 (S); *LIMC*, VII, pl. 23, Oknos 1 (part); Shapiro, *Personifications*, 179, fig. 134 (part of BD).

67, pl. 19.2 (part) ATHENS, 1699 (N 930) (CC 725). *ABV* 462.1; *Para* 203; *BAdd* 116.

68 WÜRZBURG, 359. *ABV* 471.118. *LIMC*, VI, pl. 194, Medeia 4 (part).

68 ATHENS. *ARV²* 1127.14; *Para* 453; *BCH*, 1930, pl. 24; Reinsberg, *Ehe*, 59, fig. 13 (A).

VII. FROM ABOUT 500 ONWARDS

A. INTRODUCTION

69 BOSTON, 13.195. *ABV* 35.1, 1621; *BAdd* 158; *Oxford Companion*, 778 (drawing of part of A); Robertson, *Vase-Painting*, 131, fig. 135 (part); *SES*, 27 (1990), 156, pl. 3; van Straten, *Hiera Kala*, fig. 17 (drawing); *Ta Attika*, 274.E2 (BD).

69 SYRACUSE, 26967. *AJA*, 102 (1998) 721, fig. 1 (drawing); *ARV²* 36.2, 1621; *Para* 325; *BAdd* 158; *GRBS*, 31 (1990) pl. 3B at p. 160 (drawing); *Rivista*, 20 (1996) fig. 7 (drawing); *Ta Attika*, 274.E3 (part, top of mouth).

70 ATHENS, Acr., 15214 (176). *ARV²* 17.18; *BAdd* 153; *LIMC*, IV, pl. 430, Hera 422 (part); Cygielmann, *Euphronios,* pl. 53 (drawing of A and B); Shapiro, *Tyrants*, pl. 26D (part).

71 ATHENS, Acr., 336. *ARV²* 192.105; *BAdd* 189; *LIMC*, IV, pl. 15, Eteokles 7 (I); *LIMC*, VII, pl. 542, septem 25 (part); *QuadTic*, 23 (1994) 44, figs. 9–10 (drawings of A, B and I); Schefold and Jung, *Argonauten*, 70–71, figs. 51–53 (A, B, I); Shapiro, *Myth into Art*, 92, figs. 62–63 (A, B, I).

72 ATHENS, Acr., 15190 (439). *ARV²* 859, 860.2, 1580.2, 1672; *Para* 425; *BAdd* 298; *Annali*, 15 (1993) pl. 19.1 (I); Boardman, *Greeks Overseas*, 238, fig. 281; Maas and Snyder, *Instruments*, 160, fig. 9 (part of I); Bonacasa, *Stile Severo*, pl. 6.4; Tsiaphaki, *Thraki*, 333, figs. 11a–b (I).

73 ATHENS, 1964 (CC 1066). *ARV²* 687.218.

D. THE MARATHON PAINTER

92 ATHENS, 1036 (CC 592). *ABV* 38.2, 681; *BAdd* 10; Petrakou, *Marathon*, 146, fig. 83 (A).

92, 106, 145, 163 MARATHON, 762a (once Athens, 1037 (CC 767)). *ABV* 393.18; Petrakou, *Marathon* 144, fig. 80; 15–16, fig. 1, pls. 1–3.

92 MARATHON (once Athens, 1044). *CV* 1, pl. 13 (21).5 (I); *GVGetty*, 5 (1991) 45, fig. 5 (drawing of I).

92 ATHENS, 1043 (CC 607). *CV* 1, pl. 12 (20).1–2; Lioutas, *Lekanai*, pl. 24.2; Petrakou, *Marathon*, 143, fig. 79 (I).

92 ATHENS, 1040 (CC 836). *CV* 1, pl. 10 (18).7–8 (A, B); Petrakou, *Marathon*, frontcover, 141, fig. 78 (C, colour of part of C).

E. THE SAPPHO PAINTER AND THE DIOSPHOS PAINTER

101 ATHENS, 1584 (CC 1550). *CV* 1, pl. 6 (28).1–3; Frontisi-Ducroux and Vernant, pls. 24–25 (A, B); Frontisi-Ducroux, *Masque*, 183, pl. 90; Keuls, *Phallus*, 249, figs. 224–5; *MededRome*, 9–10 (1983) pl. 4.2 (part); Moon, *Iconography*, 220, figs. 14.26A–C.

101 ATHENS, 12471 (1004). *ARV²* 302.11, 306.

101 ATHENS, 1823 (CC 1838). *ARV²* 998.169; Oakley, *Achilles Painter*, pl. 121C–D (BD); Tzachou-Alexandri, *Leukes Likythoi*, 135, fig. 38, pls. 43–46 (colour, profile).

101 ATHENS, 12746 (N 1004). *ARV²* 999.184; Oakley, *Achilles Painter*, pl. 131A–B (BD); Tzachou-Alexandri, *Leukes Likythoi*, 138, fig. 39, pls. 47–50 (colour, profile).

102.1 LONDON, B 668. *ARV²* 98.1; 102.2, 1626; *Para* 330; *BAdd* 172; Boardman, *Ceramica*, 216 (part); Lissarrague, *Guerrier*, 186, fig. 108 (drawing); Robertson, *Vase-Painting*, 53, figs. 39–40 (A, B).

102.2, 103 ATHENS, 15002. *ARV²* 98.2, 102.3, 1626; *BAdd* 172; Duby and Perrot, *Femmes*, 250, fig. 63 (drawing); Lissarrague, *Guerrier* 186, fig. 109 (drawing of A and B); *REA*, 94 (1992) 145, fig. 7 (drawing).

102.3 BOSTON, 00.358. *ARV²* 101.30, 104.19; *BAdd* 172.

102.5 TÜBINGEN, H 10/1200 (E 48). *ARV²* 100.28; 103.17; BAdd 172.

102.6 NEW YORK, 21.80. *ARV²* 99.5, 1584.15; *BAdd* 172.

102.7 PARIS, CA 1920. *ARV²* 99.3, 102.4; BAdd 172.

102.8, 103 ATHENS, 2207. *ARV²* 99.4.

102.9 NEW YORK, 06.1021.92. *ARV²* 99.6; *BAdd* 172.

105 WÜRZBURG, 436. *ABV* 294.16; *BAdd* 76.

105 ORVIETO, 293. *ABV* 613.6; *Para* 305.

105 MUNICH, 1987 (J 344). *ABV* 613.4; *Para* 305.

105 CAMBRIDGE, GR 9.1937 (once Cambridge, Ricketts and Shannon). *ABV* 611.5; *BAdd* 143; Darracott, *Ricketts and Shannon*, no. 52B.

105 BERLIN, F 2095. *ABV* 610.1; *Para* 304; *BAdd* 142; *Ausgestellte Werke*, 92, no. 4 (part).

105 COMPIEGNE, 1075. *ABV* 295.1.

105 COMPIEGNE, 1073. *ABV* 295.1; *LIMC*, V, pl. 308, Hippalektryon 75 (part).

105 MUNICH, 2003 (J 355). Berard, *Image* 122, fig. 2A; Brommer, *Herakles*, 22, pl. 13B; Brommer, *Heracles*, pl. 18; *Kunst der Schale*, 188, 266, 470, figs. 30.2.2, 42.2, no. 12 (A); Mertens, *White Ground*, pl. 12.3 (A); Schefold, *Heldensagen*, 110, fig. 124; Schefold, *Heroes*, fig. 124; Valavanis and Kourkoumelis, *Chaire*, 107 (colour of A).

108 THEBES, 6151 (R26.84). Demakopoulou and Konsola, pl. 34, bottom; *CV*, fig. 33, pls. 62.1–3, 63.4, 69.8.

108 THEBES, 6017 (R31.165). *ABV* 496.178; *CV*, pls. 65.1–3, 69.15.

111a NAPLES, 81254 (H 2763). *ARV²* 302.13; *LIMC*, VIII, pl. 760, Silenoi 82 (part).

112b SYRACUSE, 43052. *ABV* 301.8.

112c, 154, pl. 40.1A–B PARIS, MNB 911 (E 10). *ARV²* 301.1, 303; *BAdd* 211; Cesare, *Statue in Immagine*, 211, fig. 147 (part); *JHS*, 102 (1982) pl. 5C.

112α PARIS, MNC 650. *ARV²* 301.6; *Para* 356; *BAdd* 212.

112β ATHENS, 12769 (N 981). *ARV²* 302.9, 305.6.

112γ, 101 ATHENS, 12471. *ARV²* 302.11, 306.

112δ THEBES, R.46.84. *ARV²* 302.10, 306.7.

112 VIENNA (once Österreichisches Museum, 234). *ABV* 507.

112 TÜBINGEN, S 10/1366 (E 56). *ARV²* 305; *BAdd* 212.

114, 116 ATHENS, 517 (CC 971); *Para* 248; *BAdd* 127; *BCH*, 79 (1955) 190, fig. 13; Brinkmann, *Beobachtungen,* 87, fig. D (drawing of BD); *Fest Hampe*, pl. 51.1; *LIMC*, VII, 978, Kyknos I 121 (drawing); Simon, *Ausgewählte Schriften,* 106, fig. 9.5 (drawing).

116 ATHENS, Vlasto. Boardman, *Black Figure*, fig. 267 (part).

116 ATHENS, 516 (CC 970). *ABV* 508; *BCH*, 1936, 55, pls. 20–21; Brommer, *Satyrspiele,* 33; Buschor, *Satyrtänze*, fig. 57; *Modi e Funzioni*, 193–194, fig. 10 (BD).

116 OSLO, University. *Para* 248.

118 note 1 ATHENS, 2185 (CC 844); *ABV* 481.γ; *BAdd* 121.

120.7 CAMBRIDGE, GR 78.1864 (G 100). *BdA*, 30 (1936–37) 42, fig. 8; Brize, *Geryoneis*, pl. 10.2; Brommer, *Herakles II*, 106, fig. 51 (drawing); *CV* 1, pl. 22.11; *LIMC*, V, pl. 637, Helios 96; Lacroix, *Etudes*, pl. 24.

120.9 WÜRZBURG, L 384. *LIMC*, V, pl. 631, Helios 3 (part).

120.10, 123, 124 NEW YORK, GR 540. *LIMC*, V, pl. 631, Helios 7 (part).

127.2, 93, 132–133 ATHENS, 15375. *ARV²* 447.274, 1653; *BAdd* 241; Buitron-Oliver, *Douris,* pl. 56.85; *Looking at Greek Vases*, 5, fig. 1; Robertson, *Vase-Painting*, 92, fig. 85 (part).

F. THE HAIMON PAINTER AND HIS GROUP

132 ATHENS. *ABV* 540.20.

134 ATHENS Acr., 2499. *ABV* 506; *LIMC*, IV, pl. 133, Gigantes 255 (part).

136 ATHENS, Acr., 1335. *ABV* 569.673.

139 PARIS, F 454. *ABV* 547.240.

G. THE THESEUS PAINTER AND HIS GROUP

140 ATHENS, 1582. *ABV* 547.229.

140, note 2 PARIS, CabMéd, 283. *ABV* 553.390. *Para* 270.

141 THEBES, 1500 (R.46.68). *ABV* 547.246; *CV*, pls. 68.1–3, 69.21.

147, 163 ATHENS, 12394 (N 1028). *ADelt*, 36 (1981) 1, pl. 56A; *ARV²* 211.192.

156 ATHENS, 12552 (418). *ABV* 59.12; *Para* 25; *BAdd* 16; *CV* 3, pl. 11, fig. 7; Tzachou-Alexandri, *Mind and Body,* 305, no. 193 (parts of A and B).

160 BOSTON, 13.74. *ABV* 530.84; *Para* 264.

162 ATHENS, 1305 (CC 1188). *ARV²* 452.2; Tzachou-Alexandri, *Mind and Body,* 259, no.151.

162 ATHENS, 1633 (CC 1189). *ARV²* 452.4.

162 ATHENS, 12803 (N 1030). *ARV²* 452.5.

163 ATHENS, 1975 (CC 1061). Kurtz, *AWL*, pl. 20.3; *Hephaistos* 14 (1996) 89, fig. 7 (part).

164, 186 ATHENS, 1028. *CV* 1, pl. 10 (18).13.

164, 186 ATHENS, 1026. *CV* 1, pl. 10 (18).3.

164, 186 ATHENS, 1027. *CV* 1, pl. 10 (18).2.

166 ATHENS, 11050 (N 936). *AJA*, 58 (1954), pl. 59, fig. 20 (drawing); Carpenter, *Art and Myth*, fig. 37 (drawing); *DialHist*, 10 (1984) 220, fig. 13; *JHS*, 14 (1894) pl. 9 (drawing); *LIMC*, VII, pl. 410, Priamos 119 (drawing); *RA*, 50 (1957) 37, fig. 10 (drawing).

166 ATHENS, 1033. *CV* 1, pl. 10 (18).12.

157 ATHENS, 1827 (CC 1023). *ARV²* 685.181; *BAdd* 279.

I. THE WORKSHOP OF THE BELDAM PAINTER

172, note 1 ATHENS, 1958 (CC 1690). *ARV*² 748.2, 1668; *BAdd* 284; Immerwahr, *Attic Script* pl. 30.123 (part); *Para* 413.

172 ATHENS, 1935 (CC 1692). *ARV*² 1227.1; *BAdd* 350; *Para* 466; Tiverios, *Techni,* 230, fig. 216 (colour of part); Fantham, *Women,* 97, fig. 3.11; Himmelmann, *Grabreliefs,* 72, fig. 34 (BD).

177 ATHENS, 1963 (CC 1628). *ARV*² 995.122, 1574, 1677; *BAdd* 312; Oakley, *Achilles Painter,* pl. 93B–C (BD); *Para* 438; Tzachou-Alexandri, *Leukes Likythoi,* 114, fig. 30, pls. 17–20 (colour, profile).

177 ATHENS, 12440. *ARV*² 996.132, 1575; Oakley, *Achilles Painter,* pl. 99D (part of BD); Tzachou-Alexandri, *Leukes Likythoi,* 101, fig. 24, pls. 1–4 (colour, profile).

172 ATHENS, 1960 (CC 1699). *ARV*² 1228.4; *BAdd* 351.

178 ATHENS, 1696 (CC 1423). *ARV,* 712.87.

178 ATHENS, 1522 (CC 1438). *ARV*² 713.122.

178 ATHENS, 1600 (CC 1409). *ARV*² 713.123.

178 ATHENS, 1984 (CC 1064). *ARV*² 715.185.

178 ATHENS, 1988 (CC 1063). *ARV*² 715.186; *BAdd* 282.

178 ATHENS, 1978 (CC 1062). *ARV*² 715.188.

181 ATHENS, 1349 (CC 1470). *ARV*² 732.36.

181 ATHENS, 1751 (CC 1442). *ARV*² 732.38.

181 ATHENS, 1503 (CC 1465). *ARV*² 733.53.

182 LONDON, 1836.2–24.33. Kurtz, *AWL,* pl. 72.7.

182 LONDON, B 659. Kurtz, *AWL,* pl. 70.1.

182, pl. 54.3 (part) OXFORD, 1930.617. Kurtz, *AWL,* pl. 71.4.

183 ATHENS, 1725 (CC 1081). *ARV*² 726.9, 728.

183 ATHENS, 12767 (N 976). *ARV*² 728; *BAdd* 282.

183 LONDON, 1864.10–7.17. Kurtz, *AWL,* pl. 71.3.

183.III a SYRACUSE, 45988. *Ta Attika,* 323.H2 (part).

183.IV a CHIUSI, 1828. *ARV*² 930.99; *BAdd* 306.

183.IV b BERLIN, F 2606. *CV* 1, pl. 53.7–9 (A, UH).

184.VI WÜRZBURG, L 619. *AJA,* 58 (1945) 193, no. 11; *Luxusgeschirr,* 135, no. 12.2 (A).

184.VII ROME. *ARV*² 1280.67.

184–5.VIII Stemless cups, generally with lozenges on the outside; under the handle there is usually either a palmette or a small figure in silhouette:

NAPLES, 81311 (H 2621). *ARV²* 1279.49.

OXFORD, 1965.113 (once Northwick, Spencer-Churchill). *ARV²* 1279.50; *Para* 472.

LONDON, 1920.12–21.1. *ARV²* 1277.23, 1282.1, 1689; *BAdd* 357; Boardman, *Greek Art*, 272–273, fig. 277; *Pandora*, 68, fig. 11 (BD); Cavalier, *Silence et Fureur*, 414, fig. 119; Fantham, *Women*, 99–100, figs. 3.13–14; Boardman, *Classical*, fig. 243; *CAH*, *Plates to Volumes 5&6*, 132, fig. 134 (drawing of BD); Duby and Perrot, *Femmes*, 168–169, fig. 3 (drawing); Lang, *Life, Death and Litigation*, 19, fig. 23 (drawing of BD); Oakley and Sinos, *Wedding*, 92–94, figs. 75–78.

LEIPZIG, T 3585. *ARV²* 1282.4; Paul, *Sponsoren*, 73, no. 37 (colour of I).

LONDON, 1919.7–26.1. *ARV²* 1282.10.

VIENNA, 149. *ARV²* 1282.11.

SÈVRES, 250. *ARV²* 1282.12, 1297.

LEIPZIG, T 637. *ARV²* 1283.20.

TARQUINIA, RC 7458. *ARV²* 1283.21.

Two by one hand: –

ATHENS, 238 (CC 1218). *ARV²* 1290.21.

BERLIN, F 2546. *ARV²* 1291.1.

Upright feathers on the outside: –

TARQUINIA, RC 993. *ARV²* 1138.53.

185 COPENHAGEN, VIII.996 (B 175). *CV*, 3, pl. 111.21.

185 CAMBRIDGE, GR 20.1885 (G 114). *CV* 1, pl. 22.18.

185 KARLSRUHE, B 765 (once Thiersch , 439). *CV* 1, pl. 32.8.

186 ATHENS, 1035. *CV* 1, pl. 10 (18).4.

187–188, note 3 LEIDEN, PC 95 (once Canino, 751*)*. *CV* 4, 91, fig. 15, pl. 184.1–2 (A, B, profile); *AJA*, 59 (1955) pl. 36, fig. 20.

187–188, note 3 LEIDEN, PC 96 (once Canino*)*. *CV* 4, 91, fig. 16, pl. 184.3–4 (A, B, profile).

LEKYTHOI OF THE DOLPHIN CLASS

THE DOLPHIN PAINTER

193.3 COPENHAGEN, 7299. *CV* 3, pl. 109.6.

193.5 READING, 26.XII.8. *ABV* 698.3bis; *Para* 199.

THE DOLPHIN CLASS

193.9 BRUSSELS, A 2127. *CV* 2, pl. 21 (61).3.

194.15, pl. 5.4 SYRACUSE, 11398. *Para* 199.7bis.

94.18, 16, 36 ATHENS, 1093 (CC 721). *ABV* 459.

II. THE PHAROS PAINTER

194.1, 5, 25, pl. 8.1 NEW YORK, 75.2.10 (GR 541). *ABV* 698; *Para* 199.1; *Jb*, 102 (1987) 37, fig. 24B (drawing).

194.5, pl. 8.3 BERLIN, F 1738. *ABV* 456. *Jb*, 102 (1987) 37, fig. 24A (drawing); *Para* 199.5.

194.6 COPENHAGEN, 5181. *CV* 3, pl. 109.4; *LIMC*, VI, pl. 558, Nike 7; *Guides*, 99.1 (colour).

ADDENDA TO BEAZLEY'S ATTRIBUTIONS TO THE PHAROS PAINTER

OXFORD, 1946.182. *ABV* 456.1; *BAdd* 115; *Jb*, 102 (1987) 37, fig. 24C. *Para* 199.

SYRACUSE. *ABV* 456.2.

SYRACUSE. *ABV* 457.

III. THE GROUP OF THE LITTLE BLACK-NECK LEKYTHOI

195.8, 8, pl. 9.2 (part) MUNICH, 1842. *ABV* 455.

195.11 ERLANGEN, M 1100 (on permanent loan from Munich, J 636). *CV*, Munich 11, pl. 19. 1–5, Beilage 4.3; *Kunst der Schale*, 155, fig. 24. 8 (A).

195.13 LONDON, B 586. Boardman, *ABFV*, fig. 148; *JHS*, 80 (1960) pl. 3.1.

195.14, 14, 27–28, 194 BONN, 539. *ABV* 455.

195.20 NEW HAVEN, 1913.109. Burke & Pollitt, 29, no. 32.

195.21 MADRID, 10961. *CV* 1, pl. 29.1.

195.32 HEIDELBERG, L 56. *CV* 4, pl. 168.1, 2.

IV. THE WRAITH PAINTER

196.1 ATHENS, 1071 (CC 672). *ABV* 200.1

196.2, pl. 9.3 (part) SYRACUSE, 20958. *ABV* 200.2; *Ta Attika*, 250.C8 (part).

196.3, 30, pl. 9.5 (part) ATHENS, 1072 (CC 673). *ABV* 200.3.

196.4 ROME, M 554. *ABV* 200.4.

196.5, 37, pl. 11.1 (part) ATHENS, 9695. *ABV* 200.5.

196.6, 37, pls. 11.2, 12.3 (S, part of BD) ATHENS, 372 (CC 704). *ABV* 200.6.

ADDENDA TO BEAZLEY'S ADDITIONS TO THE WRAITH PAINTER

201.12, 689 MAINZ, 92. *Para* 86; Junker, *Mythos und Lebenswelt*, 38, fig. 17 (A).

201.14 CHATILLON-SUR-SEINE. *Para* 86; Haffner, *Heiligtümer*, 46, fig. 39 (colour of A); Angeli, *Hallstattkultur*, colour pl. 6, pl. 12.2 (A, colour of A); Joffroy, *Vix*, pls. 56, XI (colour); *Luxusgeschirr*, 65, fig. 2 (A).

201.17 HAVANA, 110. Olmos, *Habana*, 93–94, no.25 (A, parts).

V. THE DAYBREAK PAINTER

196.1, 57–58, 99, 120–122, pl. 17.1A–C ATHENS, 513 (CC 900). *ABV* 380.290; *Para* 163; *LIMC*, V, 81, Herakles 2545 (drawing).

196.2 CRACOW, 1245. *ABV* 380.291 (Leagros Group); *Para* 163; *BAdd* 100.

196.3, pl. 17.2. MUNICH, 1891 (J 761). *ABV* 380.292 (Leagros Group); *Para* 164.

197.5 TARANTO, 6924. *Taras, Rivista*, 10 (1990) pl. 41.3 (part).

197.6 MUNICH, 1889 (J 767), from Sicily. *ABV* 380.288, 600, 605.85 (Leagros Group, Red-Line Painter); *BAdd* 141; Holmberg, *Red-Line Painter*, 16, fig. 8 (part); *OpuscRom*, 16 (1987) 63, fig. 8 (parts); *OpuscRom*, 17 (1989) 63, fig. 4 (part).

197.7 TARANTO, 4404 (9125). Boardman, *ABFV*, fig. 231.1, 2; *Para* 213; Shapiro, *Myth into Art*, 58–59, figs. 36–37; Touchefeu-Meynier, *Thèmes Odysséens*, pl. 13.1–2; Andreae, *Ulisse*, 134, fig. 2.29 (colour of part).

197.8 SYRACUSE, 12639. *ABV* 449.8 (Painter of Rhodes 13472).

197.9, 58 ATHENS, 12951 (N 948). *ABV* 380.287.

197.10 BONN, 2052. *ABV* 380.293 (Leagros Group).

197.12 PARIS, CabMed, 257. *ABV* 363.47 (*cf.* the Painter of Sèvres 100, Leagros Group, Antiope Group); *BAdd* 97.

197.14 PARIS, F 349. *ABV* 427.24 (Keyside Class).

197.15, pl. 17.3 BOSTON, 03.783. *ABV* 378.252 (Leagros Group); *BAdd* 100; *LIMC*, V, pl. 92, Herakles 2550.

197.16 BOLOGNA, 62. *ABV* 449.3 (Painter of Rhodes 13472).

197.17 RHODES, 13472. *ABV* 449.4 (Painter of Rhodes 13472).

197.18 RHODES, 12299. *ABV* 449.2 (Painter of Rhodes 13472).

197.19 BOLOGNA, 17352 (63). *ABV* 534.10 (Leagros Group, Painter of Sèvres 100); *Para* 266; Berti, and Gasparri, 39.7.

197.20 RHODES, 13472. *ABV* 449.1 (Painter of Rhodes 13472); *Para* 195; *BAdd* 114; *Potters and Painters*, 460, fig. 4 (BD); Schmitt Pantel, *Banquet*, fig. 22.

Close to the Daybreak Painter

198 COPENHAGEN, 3629. *ABV* 379.272 (Leagros Group); *BAdd* 100.

198 MADRID, 10904 (L 67). *ABV* 363.41, 359 (Group of Vatican 424, Leagros Group).

VI. THE CACTUS PAINTER

198.2, pl. 18.1 (part) BERLIN, 3261. *ABV* 472; Boardman, *ABFV*, fig. 233; Brommer, *Herakles,* pl. 28b; Brommer, *Heracles,* pl. 43; Carpenter, *Art and Myth,* fig. 211 (part); Immerwahr, *Attic Script* pl. 25.105 (part); Kurtz, *AWL*, pl. 4.3; *LIMC*, V, pl. 102, Herakles 2692; Grabow, *Schlangenbilder*, pl. 18.K87 (part).

198.4 OXFORD, 1895.75 (V 512). *Para* 212; Kurtz, *AWL*, pl. 4.4.

198.5 ATHENS, private. *JHS*, 106 (1986) 62, fig. 1 (drawing); Prag, *Oresteia*, pl. 29A (drawing); Grabow, *Schlangenbilder*, pl. 22.K104 (drawing).

198.6, 62, 76, pl. 18.5 (part) ATHENS, 12821. *ABV* 505; *BAdd* 126; Prag, *Oresteia*, pl. 28d.

198.7, 62, pl. 18.2 HEIDELBERG, 257. *ABV* 451.8, 472.

VII. 'THE PHANYLLIS' CLASS

A. THE PHANYLLIS PAINTER

(a) Broad Phanyllis-shaped

199.1 DELOS, B 6.136 (548). Dugas, *Delos* X, pl. 41.548; *Muse,* 23/24 (1989/90) 51, fig. 3 (part)

199.2 SYRACUSE, 2365. Giudice, *Phanyllis,* pls. 1.2, 6, 13.2.

199.3 GELA, N 38 (once Gela, Navarra). *CV* 3, pl. 6.1–2, 4.

199.4 AGRIGENTO, 864 (6). *CV* 1, pl. 39.1–2; Giudice, *Phanyllis,* pls. 1.3, 7, 13.4.

199.5 AGRIGENTO, 863. *CV* 1, pl. 39.3–4; Giudice, *Phanyllis,* pls. 1.4, 8, 13.5.

199.6 ATHENS, 12776 (N 945). Giudice, *Phanyllis,* 52, fig. 7 (drawing).

199.7 LEIDEN, K 94.9.29. *CV* 2, pl. 89.1; Giudice, *Phanyllis,* pl. 13.3 (S).

199.8 CORINTH, MP 121. Giudice, *Phanyllis,* 54, fig. 2 (drawing). *Hesperia,* 58 (1989) pl. 65,90.

199.9 SYRACUSE, 21942. Giudice, *Phanyllis,* pls. 3.1–3, 13.6.

199.10 VIENNA, 181. Giudice, *Phanyllis,* pls. 2.3, 3.4–5, 13.7.

(β) Cylinders

199.13 TARANTO, 20314 (20324) (9887). *Atti e Memorie della Societa Magna Grecia,* NS 8 (1967) pl. 23A–C; *LIMC,* VI, pl. 24, Kirke 5; *Para* 204; Touchefeu-Meynier, *Thèmes Odysséens,* pl. 13.3–5; Andreae, *Ulisse,* 134, fig. 2.30 (colour of part).

199.16 SYRACUSE, 2342. Giudice, *Phanyllis,* pls. 7.2, 7–8, 14.7.

200.17 SYRACUSE, 2343. Giudice, *Phanyllis,* pls. 7.1, 5–6, 14.6.

200.18 SYRACUSE, 2344. Giudice, *Phanyllis,* pls. 6.1–4, 14.5.

200.19 SYRACUSE, 2345. *AM,* 89 (1974) pl. 43.1; Giudice, *Phanyllis,* pls. 5.1–4, 14.4.

200.21 COPENHAGEN, Ny Carlsberg, 2658. Johansen, F., *Greece in the Archaic Period, Catalogue Ny Carlsberg Glyptotek* (Copenhagen, 1994) 103, no. 193; *LIMC,* I, pl. 302, Aineias 86.

200.22 MUNICH, 1886 (1332). Giudice, *Phanyllis,* pls. 9.1–4, 14.10.

200.24 LENTINI, 2616 (once Palazzolo Acreide, Iudica). Giudice, *Phanyllis,* pls. 2.1, 4, 13.11.

200.25 VIENNA, 712. Giudice, *Phanyllis,* pls. 2.2, 5, 13.12.

200.26 LONDON, B 529. *ABV* 490.25; Giudice, *Phanyllis,* I, 80, figs. 6–7 (drawings); *LIMC*, VII, pl. 688, Kyknos I11 (part); *Para* 223.

200.27 LONDON, B 559. *ABV* 496.161; *Para* 223; Giudice, *Phanyllis*, pl. 11.2, 4.

200.28 TARANTO, 1690. *Para* 227.

200.30 LONDON, B 564. *ABV* 497.189; Giudice, *Phanyllis,* 59, fig. 3 (drawing)

200.31 PALERMO, 1215 (1902). Giudice, *Phanyllis,* pls. 8.1–2, 14.8.

200.32 LONDON, 1867.5–8.983 (B 284). *ABV* 592.2 (Painter of Würzburg 232); *BAdd* 140.

200.33 WÜRZBURG, 232. *ABV* 592.1 (Painter of Würzburg 232).

200.34 LONDON, B 281. *ABV* 606.13; *Para* 302; *Ta Attika,* 299.F68 (A, B).

200.35 GENEVA, I 36.1874 (I 36). *CV* 2, pl. 54.1–3.

200.36 PARIS, F 395. *ABV* 592.5 (Group of Oxford 216); *BAdd* 140.

200.37 MANNHEIM, CG 40. *ABV* 603.51 (Red-Line Painter).

200.38 FRANKFURT, MusVF, β 290. *ABV* 592 (Near the painter of Würzburg 232); *Para* 297; *CV* 1, pl. 34.3–4 (A, B).

200.39 COPENHAGEN, VIII318 (65). *ABV* 504, 593.1 (Class of Athens 581, Kalinderu Group).

200.40 AMSTERDAM, 1847. *ABV 593.3* (Near the painter of Würzburg 232).

200.41 ROME, 1444. *ABV* 436.5 (Painter of Brussels R 236); *Para* 188.

200.42 PARIS, F 327. *Para* 190.7 (Class of Vatican G 50).

NEAR THE PHANYLLIS PAINTER

201 GENEVA, MF 236. *Acta Iranica,* 23 (1984) pl. 4, fig. 7 (A); Bruxelles, *Palais des Beaux-Arts, Hommes et Dieux de la Grèce Antique* (1.10–2.12.1982) 69, no. 23 (A, B); *CV* 2, pl. 51.1–4.

B. THE GROUP OF 'ARMING' LEKYTHOI

(a) With various subjects

201.2 PALERMO, 1928 (1188). Giudice, *Phanyllis,* 24.1–2, 5–6, 32.11.

201.3 THEBES, 6147 (R.80.234). Giudice, *Phanyllis,* pls. 24.3, 7–8, 32.12; *CV,* pls. 61.1–3, pl. 69.11.

201.5 VIENNA, 87. Giudice, *Phanyllis,* pls. 20.2, 7–8, 32.4.

201.6 GELA, N 37. *CV* 1, pls. 4.1–2, 4, 5.1.

201.10 (?) AGRIGENTO, C 1552 (292). *CV* 1, pls. 40.1–2, 42.1.

201.11 PALERMO, 1825 (1189). Giudice, *Phanyllis*, pls. 18.4, 19.3, 32.1.

201.12 PALERMO, 1833 (57). Giudice, *Phanyllis*, 26.1–2, 33.3.

201.13 ADRIA, 23877 (1107) (A 63). *CV* 2, pl. 23.3.5 (S, BD); Giudice, *Phanyllis*, pls. 25.2, 33.1.

201.14 PALERMO, 1827 (58). Giudice, *Phanyllis*, pls. 28 1, 5, 33; *Ta Attika*, 261.D23 (parts).

201.15 BRISTOL, 1827 (804). Giudice, *Phanyllis*, pls. 28.4, 8, 33.9.

201.16 VIENNA, 209. Giudice, *Phanyllis*, pls. 28.2, 6, 33.7.

201.17 TARANTO, 8.7.1921. *ABV* 464; *CV* 1, pl. 12.1.

202.18 SYRACUSE, 7484/A. Giudice, *Phanyllis*, pls. 18.1, 5, 6, 31.10.

(β) With the 'Arming' scene

202.20 FLORENCE, 3796. Giudice, *Phanyllis*, pls. 15.3, 8, 31.3.

202.21 THEBES, 6135 (R.80.232) (E 121.80). Giudice, *Phanyllis*, pls. 15.1, 5–6, 31.1; *CV*, pls. 60.4–6, 63.3, 69.10, fig. 32.

202.22, 55 VIENNA, 154. Giudice, *Phanyllis*, pls. 15.4, 16.5, 31.4.

202.23 SYRACUSE, 24676. Giudice, *Phanyllis*, pls. 15.2, 7, 31.2.

202.24 CAMBRIDGE, GR 6.1917. Boardman, *ABFV*, fig. 237; *CV* 1, pl. 22.26.

202.26 VIENNA, 208. Giudice, *Phanyllis*, pls. 16.1, 7, 31.5.

202.28 OXFORD, 1938.908. *ABV* 464.

202.29 (?) AGRIGENTO, C 839. *CV* 1, pls. 40.3–4, 42.2.

202.30 VIENNA, 711. Giudice, *Phanyllis*, pls. 17.1, 5, 31.9; Bernhard-Walcher, *Antikes Leben*, 62, no. 12 (part).

202.31 READING, 25.VIII.1. *CV* 1, pl. 12.1.

202.32 VIENNA, 666. Giudice, *Phanyllis*, pls. 16.4, 17.4, 31.8.

Probably by the same Painter

202, 65 PARIS, ED 17 (L 16). Giudice, *Phanyllis*, 71, fig. 4 (drawing).

LEKYTHOI CONNECTED WITH THE PHANYLLIS AND ARMING GROUPS

From the Phanyllis Workshop (in Phanyllis shape)

203.3 KARLSRUHE, B 2319 (179). *CV* 1, pl. 32.7.

***Lekythoi between those of the Phanyllis Painter and the 'Arming'
Lekythoi(cylinder-shaped)***

203.1 SYRACUSE, 2337. Giudice, *Phanyllis,* pls. 19.2, 5, 32.2.

203.2 SYRACUSE, 7685. Giudice, *Phanyllis,* pls. 18.3, 19.4, 31.12.

In the manner of the Phanyllis Painter (Phanyllis-shaped)

203.3 BRUSSELS, A 2191. *ABV* 699; *BAdd* 116.

203.4 PALERMO, 1898 (60). Giudice, *Phanyllis,* pls. 8.3–4, 14.9

In the manner of the 'Arming' Painter (Phanyllis-shaped)

203.3 NEWARK, 50.288 (once Paris, market). *ABV* 464; *Worcester Art Museum
Annual* 2 (1936) 25.2; *The Museum* (Newark, N.J.) 3, 6, fig. 4.2.

One outlier, somewhat better than the 'Arming' Lekythoi

(of Phanyllis shape; smallish)

203 SYRACUSE, 2338. Giudice, *Phanyllis,* pls. 23.1–4, 32.10.

C. THE CHARIOT PAINTER

203.1, 65–66, 106, pl. 19.4A–B ATHENS, 2246. Kurtz, *AWL,* pl. 4.1; *Para* 206.

204.4 ELEUSIS, 566 (949). *Para* 206.

204.5 SYRACUSE, 2335. Giudice, *Phanyllis,* pls. 30.1–5, 33.12.

204.8 ATHENS, 456 (CC 732). *CV* 1, pl. 6 (14).1–2.

204.9 ATHENS, 457 (CC 733). *CV* 1, pl. 6 (14).3–4.

NEAR THE CHARIOT PAINTER

204.4 CAMBRIDGE, GR 5.1937 (once Ricketts and Shannon). *CV* 2, pl. 1.2.

D. LEKYTHOI WITH A SINGLE UPRIGHT PALMETTE BETWEEN TWO ANIMALS, ON THE SHOULDER

204.1 SYRACUSE, 23156. Giudice, *Phanyllis,* pls. 46.1–4, 51.7–8.

204.2 SYRACUSE. Giudice, *Phanyllis,* pl. 46.6.

204.3 SYRACUSE. Giudice, *Phanyllis,* pl. 46.5.

204.4 LONDON, B 537. *LIMC*, VI, pl. 554, Nessos 121; *Ta Attika*, 263.D28 (parts).

E. LEKYTHOI WITH A SINGLE UPRIGHT PALMETTE, BETWEEN TWO ONLOOKERS, ON THE SHOULDER

(the class of 'hoplite leaving home')

(α) Normal, selected from published examples

205.4 COPENHAGEN, 1938. *CV* 3, pl. 109.7.

205.5 COPENHAGEN. *CV* 3, pl. 109.8.

205.7 ROME, 50514 (561). Giudice, *Phanyllis,* pls. 37.2, 6, 48.5.

(β) Variations

205.2 GELA, 40212 (67) (N 4). *CV* 3, pls. 8.3–4, 10.3–4; Giudice, *Phanyllis,* pl. 40.1, 5, 49.3; *Ta Attika*, 262.D27 (part).

205.3 SYRACUSE, 44075. Giudice, *Phanyllis,* pls. 38.3, 7, 48.9; *Para* 214.2; *BAdd* 118.

205.4 PARIS, Petit Palais, 433. *ABV* 466.

VIII. THE GELA PAINTER

82 COLOGNY, Bodmer. *ABV* 478.8; *BAdd* 121; *LIMC*, IV, pl. 352, Helene 335 (B).

DIVISION I

205.1 AGRIGENTO, 63 (once Giudice). *Para* 214.1; *BAdd* 118; *Ta Attika*, D34 (part).

205.2 AGRIGENTO, R 145 (67) (once Giudice). Boardman, *ABFV,* fig. 234; *CV* 1, pl. 53; *LIMC*, VI, pl. 18, Kerkopes 20 (part); De Miro, *Templi*, 69, fig. 74 (part); *Ta Attika*, 264.D35 (part).

DIVISION IIa

206.3, pl. 23.3 PALERMO, 2023. Berard, *Anodoi*, pl. 5, fig. 11; *Cité des Images,* 150, fig. 212; Immerwahr, *Attic Script* pl. 25.104 (part); *LIMC*, III, pl. 298, Dionysos 27 (part); *Looking at Greek Vases*, 110, fig. 45; Mertens, *White Ground*, pl. 35.1; *REA*, 90 (1988) 1–2, 58, fig. 9; Rizza, *Sicilia*, I, 198, fig. 14.

206.5, 120.4, pl. 23.1 (part) BOSTON, 93.99. *AJA*, 84 (1980) pl. 40, fig. 14 (part); *AM*, 87 (1972) pl. 44.1. *LIMC*, V, pl. 631, Helios 2.

206.7 CAMBRIDGE, GR 52.1864 (G 75).

206.9 TÜBINGEN, S 666 (D 69). *CV* 3, pl. 46.5–7, 49.2; *LIMC*, III, pl. 338, Dionysos 364 (part).

206.14 SYRACUSE, 21156. *Ta Attika,* 265.D41 (part).

206.16, 80, 84, pl. 24.1 (part) VIENNA, 198. *Acta Hungaricae*, 30 (1982–84) fig. 5 at 64 (part).

206.17 GELA, 40218 (N 126.B) (once Gela, Navarra). *CV* 3, pls. 13.3–4, 14.2, 15.3–4; *Ta Attika*, 265.D42 (parts); *Ta Attika*, 265.D42 (parts).

DIVISION IIb

207.35 ATHENS, Agora, P 1331. *ABV* 473; *Hesperia* 15 (1946) pl. 50.119.

207.36 GELA, 40217 (N 40) (once Gela, Navarra). *CV* 3, pls. 13.1–2, 14.1, 15.1–2; *Ta Attika*, 266.D46 (parts).

DIVISION IIc

207.43 ZURICH, 2478, 2334. *CV* 1, pls. 18.4–6, 19.6; *LIMC*, VIII, pl. 442, Kentauroi et Kentaurides 240A; *Ta Attika*, 266–267.D47 (BD).

207.45, 84 SYRACUSE, 10786. Sakowski, *Dreifußkessel*, 395, fig. 38 (part).

207.46 NAPLES, 81190 (H 2464) (M 1001). *BABesch*, 49 (1974) 141, figs. 42, 43; Durand, *Sacrifice*, 93, fig. 18E (drawing); Rizza, *Sicilia*, I, 193, fig. 5 (drawing).

207.47 CRACOW, University, 1242 (288). *CV*, pl. 7 (80).6A–B; Schnapp, *Chasseur* 245, no. 171 (drawing).

207.48 SYRACUSE, 21941. *Ta Attika,* 267.D48 (part).

208.49, 80, pls. 23.2A–B, 27.2 ATHENS, 541 (CC 998); *BAdd* 118; Boardman, *ABFV,* fig. 235.1, 2; *Para* 214.49, 215.

208.50 TARANTO, 52320. *Taranto* I.3, 311, no. 94.1 (part).

208.51 TARANTO, 87. *Taranto* I,2, 41, figs. 7–9.

DIVISION IIIa

208.55, 81 ATHENS, 11749. *AM*, 53 (1928) BEILAGE 28.5; *Para* 214.55.

208.56 TARANTO, 6250 (5081). *Para* 215; *LIMC*, VIII, pl. 767, Silenoi 125 (part); Trendall & Webster, 26, fig. 1,18.

208.57 SYRACUSE, 26750. *Ta Attika*, 267.D49 (parts).

208.59 SYRACUSE, 21139. *Ta Attika*, 268.D50 (part).

208.60 LONDON, B 543. *LIMC*, III, pl. 54, Automedon 16 (part); *Ta Attika*, 268.D51 (parts).

208.61 SYRACUSE, 2353. *Ta Attika*, 269.D52 (part).

208.65, 79, 81, pl.25.3 PALERMO, 45. *Ta Attika*, 269.D53 (parts).

208.69 GELA, 40219 (N 43). *CV* 3, pl. 16.1–3, 5; Panvini, *Gelas*, pl. 30 (colour of part); *Ta Attika*, 270.D56 (parts); Panvini, *Gelas*, 71, pl. 30; Panvini, *Museo*, 395, VIII.43.

209.76 COPENHAGEN, 13788. *CV* 8, pl. 329.1; *Ktema*, 15 (1990) pl. 1.1 at p. 154 (part); *LIMC*, VI, pl. 629, Odysseus 110; Lund & Rasmussen. 103, fig. 2 (colour of part); *Nationalmuseets Arbejdsmark*, 1968, 47, fig. 5.

209.77 AMSTERDAM, 3741 (once Lucerne, Market). *Para* 216; *BABesch*, 49 (1974) 117–120, 156, figs. 1, 2, 5, 15–18; Vanhove, *deporte* 28, No.143 (parts); Vanhove, *Sport* 280, no. 143 (parts); *Mythen, Mensen en Muziek*, 12, fig. 24 (part).

209.78 TÜBINGEN, 34.5738. *BABesch*, 49 (1974) 142–143, figs. 44–47; *CV* 3, pl. 46.1–4; *Cité des Images*, 53, fig. 79, top right (drawing); Durand, *Sacrifice*, 93, fig. 18B (drawing); Rizza, *Sicilia*, I, 192, fig. 4 (drawing of BD).

209.80 CATANIA, 4069 (once Benedettini). Barresi and Valestro, 30, no.9 (colour of parts of BD).

209.81, pl. 24.4 (part) BOSTON, 99.526. Kurtz, *AWL*, pl. 17.2; Scheibler, *Töpferkunst*, 141, fig. 123 (part). Scheibler, *Töpferkunst2*, 141, fig. 123 (part); *Ta Attika*, 271.D60 (BD).

209.84 OXFORD, G 230 (V 514). *BABesch*, 49 (1974) 147, figs. 52–54; Durand, *Sacrifice*, 97, fig. 21A–C; Prag, *Oresteia*, pl. 42E (drawing); *Ta Attika*, 271.D61 (parts).

209.85 PARIS, Villard (once Paris, market). *ABV* 473.

DIVISION IIIb

209.89 STETTIN (once Karlsruhe, A. Vogell). *ABV* 473

209.96 AMSTERDAM, 8196 (once Six, 16). *BABesch*, 49 (1974) 117–119, 121–122, figs. 1, 2, 4, 10–14; Durand, *Sacrifice*, 93, fig. 18C (drawing); Rizza, *Sicilia*, I, 194, fig. 8 (drawing of BD).

209.97 ATHENS, Agora, P 1269. *ABV* 473; *Hesperia* 15 (1946) pl. 49.117.

210.98 DELOS, 571. Hadjidakis, *Delos,* 356, no. 690.

210.99 SYRACUSE, 21858. *Ta Attika*, 272.D66 (drawing of BD).

210.100 HAMBURG, 1899.96 (81); *Para* 214.100; *BAdd* 119; *CV* 1, pls. 29.7, 30.1–3.

210.101 ATHENS, Agora, P 2569. *ABV* 473; *Hesperia*, 15 (1946) pls. 49–50.118.

210.102 AGRIGENTO, R 149 (once Giudice 128). *CV* 1, pls. 55.1–2, 57.1.

210.105 LONDON, B 528. *LIMC*, V, pl. 133, Herakles 3040 (parts).

210.106 TARANTO, 4429 (46). *Taranto* I.3, 307, no. 85.1 (BD).

210.109 TARANTO, 4426 (46). *Taranto* I.3, 307, no. 84.1 (parts).

210.117 AGRIGENTO, C 845. *CV* 1, pls. 55.3–4, 57.2.

210.118 ATHENS, Agora, P 1343. *ABV* 473; *Hesperia*, 15 (1946) pl. 50.120.

211.132 BOLOGNA, C 96. *ABV* 473.

211.133 MADRID, 19519. *CV* 1, pl. 29.7A–B.

211.135 PARIS, CabMéd, 285 (I 4918). *CV* 2, pl. 79.18.

DIVISION IIIc

211.139 DELOS, 554. Hadjidakis, *Delos,* 356, no. 691.

211.141 CATANIA, 4080 (once Museo Biscari, 678). Barresi and Valastro, 31, no.10 (colour of BD).

211.142 NAPLES, 86324 (HRC 238). *ABV* 701.90BIS (Class Athens 581).

212.149 COMPIEGNE, 1043. *BABesch*, 49 (1974) 149, fig. 59; *CV,* pl. 12.19.

DIVISION IV

212.150 AGRIGENTO. *BAdd* 119; *Para* 214.150.

212.151, pls. 26.3A–B, 27.4 SYRACUSE, 19854. Kurtz, *AWL*, pl. 16.4; *Ta Attika*, 272.D70 (part).

212.152, pl. 26.2A–B BAGHDAD (once London, Market, Spink). *ABV* 473.

212.153 SAN SIMEON, 9900 (once Paris, market). *ABV* 473.

212.158, 79, 82, 83, 84, pl. 26.1A–C VIENNA, 84. Boardman, *ABFV*, fig. 236; Kurtz, *AWL*, pl. 17.3; *LIMC*, V, pl. 139, Herakles 3129; Thone, *Nike*, pl. 1.A–C (parts).

Indeterminate lekythoi

213.166 HONOLULU, 3594 (once Paris, market, Mikas). *ABV* 699.8bis; *Para* 214.166.

Fragments

213.167 ATHENS, Agora, P 2648. *ABV* 473; *BAdd* 119; Wolf, *Herakles*, fig. 56.

Small Neck-amphorae

213.177, 120.5 VIENNA, 815. *LIMC*, II, pl. 678, Astra 61 (A); *MittIran*, 12 (1979) pl. 42, fig. 2 (A); Schauenburg, *Helios*, fig. 22 (A).

213.178 BERLIN, F 1882. *BABesch*, 49 (1974) 147, figs. 55–56; *CV* 5, pl. 46.5–7; Cook, *Zeus*, III, 582, fig. 407 (drawing of A); Durand, *Sacrifice*, 96, fig. 19 (A).

214.180 NEW YORK, 06.1021.79. *Ta Attika*, 193, fig.1 (colour of part).

214.181 LONDON, B 498. *AK*, 32 (1989) pl. 25.4 (part); *LIMC*, V, pl. 142, Herakles 3184.

214.182 BRUSSELS, A 1903. *ABV* 473; *LIMC*, V, pl. 127, Herakles 2977.

214.185 MUNICH, 1824 (J 1335). *ABV* 473; *BAdd* 119; Aktseli, *Altäre*, pl. 11.1 (part of BD); *CV* 12, pls. 48–49, BEILAGE 17.1 (including profile); Rizza, *Sicilia*, I, 194, fig. 10 (part of BD).

214.187 LONDON, 1842.7–28.787 (B 509). *ABV* 473; *Para* 214; *CAH, Plates to Volumes 5&6*, 160, fig. 171 (BD); Green and Handley, *Theatre*, 18, no. 3 (colour of part).

214.188 PARIS, F 351. *BABesch*, 49 (1974) 154, fig. 67; *RA* (1983) 256, fig. 10; *REA*, 90 (1988) 1–2, 55, fig. 4.

214.192 NAPLES, 81185 (H 2751). *ABV* 473.

214.196, pl. 25.6 ATHENS, Vlasto. *ABV* 473.

214.197 PARIS, F 322. *ABV* 445.12; *Veder Greco* 162–163, no.41.

215.198 ROME, 20915. *BABesch*, 49 (1974) 152–153, figs. 64–66; Mertens, *White Ground*, pl. 9.4; Rizza, *Sicilia*, I, 196, fig. 11 (BD).

215.199, 79.13 PARIS, CP 96BIS (F 371). Fournier-Christol, *Olpes*, pls. 28, 35, no. 46.

215.202 PARIS, F 333. *DdA*, 1 (1979) 21, fig. 3.

215.203, 83 PARIS, F 334 (N 2635). *ABV* 473; *BABesch*, 49 (1974) 155, fig. 68; Fournier-Christol, *Olpes*, pls. 30, 34, no.48; *Para* 214; Rizza, *Sicilia*, I, 197, fig. 13 (BD).

LEKYTHOI CONNECTED WITH THE GELA PAINTER

GROUP A

215.1 SYRACUSE, 21190. *Para* 214.4 (Capodimonte Group).

215.2 GELA, 40216 (N 116). *CV* 3, pls. 11.1–2, 12.1–2; *Ta Attika*, 273.D71 (parts).

GROUP B

215.5 GELA, N 11. *CV* 3, pls. 11.3–4, 12.3–4; *Ta Attika*, 273.D72 (part).

215.8 BRUSSELS, R 271. *Para* 540.24.

ADDENDA TO BEAZLEY'S ATTRIBUTIONS TO THE GELA PAINTER

474.6 PARIS, CP 10829. *Para* 214; *BAdd* 119; Berard, *Images et société*, 140, figs. 1A–B; *RA* (1983) 249, fig. 8.

474.14 GLASGOW, Sir William Burrell Collection, 19.14. *CV*, pl. 23.12–14.

474.15 GLASGOW, Sir William Burrell Collection, 19.95. *BAdd* 119. *CV*, pl. 22.10–13.

700.16BIS BASEL, MM., *BAdd* 119. *MM*, 16 (1956) pl. 27.109. *Para* 215. *RA* (1982) 60, fig. 2; Schnapp, *Chasseur*, 245, no. 172 (drawing of BD).

474.17 NEW YORK, Spalding. *Anz*, 1978, 511, fig. 19 (drawing).

474.18 LOST. *Kölner Jahrbuch*, 28 (1995) 18, fig. 19 (part).

474.21 RUVO, 1594. Andreassi, *Jatta di Ruvo*, 121 bottom centre (colour of part).

474.23 FERRARA, 193. *BAdd* 119. Berti and Gasparri, 103.44.

475.24 FERRARA, 196. *BAdd* 119. Berti and Gasparri, 105.45; Rebecchi, *Spina*, fig. 8 at p. 176 (part).

475.27 COPENHAGEN, 69. *BAdd* 119. *CV* 3, pl. 123.3. Lund & Rasmussen, 195, fig. 2.2 (colour of part). *Para* 215.

475.29, 443.3 LONDON, 1905.7–11.1. *ABV* 443.3, 475.29; *BAdd* 120, 215. *REA*, 99 (1997) 2, 84, fig. 1 (drawing). Rizza, *Sicilia*, I, 192, fig. 1 (drawing of BD).

475 GENEVA, 12048. *Para* 214.9; *BAdd* 120; *CV* 2, pl. 73. 14–16; *La musique*, pls. 14–15.63 (parts).

475.2 FERRARA, 194. *BAdd* 120.

LOS ANGELES, Merlo, X 65.103.43. *Para* 215; *BAdd* 119; *LIMC*, V, pl. 256, Hermes 696 (part); *MM*, Sonderliste G (1964) 23, no. 24.

TARANTO, 6250. *Para* 215; *LIMC*, VIII, pl. 767, Silenoi 125 (part); Trendall & Webster, 26, fig. 1, 18.

GELA, 12356. *Para* 215; *Ta Attika*, 264–265.D39 (parts).

GIESSEN, 103. *Para* 216; *CV* 1, pl. 21.1–5, BEILAGE 3.2 (including profile).

ATHENS, 18568. *Para* 216; *BAdd* 119; Rizza, *Sicilia*, I, 192, fig. 2 (drawing of BD).

SALERNO, 5332. *Para* 216; *BAdd* 119; *AK*, 12 (1969) pl. 31.

ATHENS, Agora, P 24535. *Para* 216.

AMSTERDAM, 3742 (once Basel, Market). *Para* 216; *BAdd* 119; *MededAPM*, 18, fig. 12; *MededAPM*, 68 (1997) 1, fig. 1 (part); Rizza, *Sicilia*, I, 197, fig. 12.

IX. VASES BY THE EDINBURGH PAINTER

216.1, 87, pl. 27.5 (S) LONDON, 1899.2–18.67. *ABV* 700; *AJA*, 58 (1954) pl. 58.15 (part).

216.2, pl. 29.2 (part) OXFORD, 1890.27 (V 250); *BAdd* 120; *Apollo*, 117 (APRIL 1983) 278, fig. 4 (drawing); Beck, *Album*, pl. 61.314; Boardman, *ABFV*, fig. 239.1, 2; *Para* 217.2; Vanhove, *Sport* 169, no. 22 (colour); Rizza, *Sicilia*, I, 186, fig. 5 (drawing of BD); Vickers, *Vases*, fig. 31; Vickers, *Pottery*, 34, no. 22 (colour of part); *Annali* 4 (1997) 120, fig. 12 (part); Fisher & Wees, 361, fig. 21C (part of BD); *Ta Attika*, 279.F4bis (part).

216.3 VIENNA, 194. *Cité des Images*, 72, fig. 103 (colour); *DdA*, 1 (1979) 50–52, figs. 11–13; Schnapp, *Chasseur* 219, no.89 (BD); Bernhard-Walcher, *Antikes Leben*, 53, 82, no. 3 (including colour of part).

216.7 EDINBURGH, 1872.23.12. *CV* 1, pl. 13.9–12.

216.10 SYRACUSE, 19882. *BdA*, 31 (1937–38) 267–268, figs. 1–2 (including graffito); *Ta Attika*, 279.F4 (part).

216.11 PARIS, MusRodin, 954. *ABV* 476; *CV*, pls. 14. 9, 15.

216.17 SYRACUSE, 21153. *ABV* 666, 670; *BAdd* 147; *Ta Attika*, 279.F6 (parts).

217.18 SYRACUSE, 21135. *Ta Attika*, 280.F7 (parts).

217.19 EDINBURGH, L 224.379. *Para* 217.19; *BAdd* 120.

217.20 OXFORD, 1892.36 (V 246). Boardman, *ABFV,* fig. 242 (part).

217.24 PARIS, CA 545. *ABV* 476; *MededAPM,* 41 (1987) 18, fig. 4 (drawing).

217.26 BASEL, BS 1921.337. *CV* 1, pl. 55.1.4.

217.27, 87, 89, 158, pl. 29.3 ATHENS, 1130 (CC 958). *ABV* 476; *Para* 217; *BAdd* 120; Janni, *Mare,* 202, fig. 36 (colour of part); *LIMC,* VI, pl. 632, Odysseus 153; *Meddelelser,* 44 (1988) 137, fig. 23; Andreae, *Ulisse,* 57, fig. 15 (colour drawing).

217.28, 88–89, pl. 28 ATHENS, 550. *ABV* 476; *BAdd* 120; *Mind and Body,* 149, no.37; Shapiro, *Myth into Art,* 104, figs. 70–72.

217.31 LONDON, 1878–1.20 (B 640). Knittlmayer, *Demokratie,* pl. 18.1 (part); *LIMC,* I, Achilleus 228; *LIMC,* VII, pl. 346, Polyxene 7 (parts).

217.32, 89 TARANTO, 4422 (32). *Taranto* I.3, 313, no. 97.1 (part).

217.33, 88–9, pl. 29.5. SYRACUSE, 26832. *Ta Attika,* 280.F8 (part).

217.34 MONTREAL. *Para* 217.34.

217.36 BERKELEY, 8.16 (836). Anderson & West, 58–59, no.47; *CV* 1, pls. 27.1, 28.1.

217.38 SYRACUSE, 18418. *ABV* 476.

218.39 TARANTO, 4428 (22). *Taranto* I.3, 154, no. 10.1 (BD).

218.44 LEIDEN, VST 27 (II.1709). *CV* 2, pl. 103.1–4.

218.45 PALERMO, 144 (1884). *Ta Attika,* 281.F10 (BD).

218.46 GELA, 40221 (N 125). *ABV* 476; *Ta Attika,* 281.F11 (BD).

218.47 GELA, 40220 (N 31). *ABV* 476; Cesare, *Statue in Immagine,* 213, fig. 150 (drawing); *LIMC,* VII, pl. 679, Kassandra I 91 (parts); Panvini, *Gelas,* pl. 39 (colour of part); Grabow, *Schlangenbilder,* pl. 19.K92 (BD); *Ta Attika,* 282.F12 (BD).

218.48, 89, 152, pl. 29.1 PALERMO, 140. *Ta Attika,* 282.F13 (BD).

218.49, 87, 88.4, 89.2 MUNICH, 1905 (J 772). *Kunst der Schale,* 471, no. 21 (part); *LIMC,* VI, pl. 549, Nessos 81; Schiffler, *Typologie des Kentauren,* pl. 2, A78; *Veder Greco,* 107, no.9.

218.51 CATANIA, 4108 (once Biscari, 692). Barresi and Valastro, 29, no. 8 (colour of BD).

218.54 TARANTO, 4574. *ABV* 476; *MededAPM,* 41 (1987) 17, figs. 3a–b; *Taranto* I.3, 7, 154, no. 9.2 (BD); *Ostraka* 6 (1997) 367, fig. 8 (part).

218.55, 56 KARLSRUHE, 185. *ABV* 476; *CV* 1, pl. 12.1–3; *LIMC,* III, pl. 391, Dionysos 775 (part).

219.64 LONDON, B 188. *CV* 3, pl. 45.10a–b. Kurtz, *AWL,* pl. 7.1; Polacco, *Teatro di Siracusa,* fig. 165 (A).

219.65 LONDON, 1856.12–26.220 (WT 220). Boardman, *ABFV,* fig. 243 (B); *CV* 3, pl. 45.6a–b; *LIMC,* V, pl. 208, Hermes 104 (A); Nick, *Parthenos,* pl. 8.2 (B).

219.66 ALTENBURG, 207. *Para* 217.66.

219.67 NEW YORK, 56.49.1. *Para* 217.67.

219.68 SCHWERIN, 726 (1264). *CV,* pls. 12.1, 2, 13.1, 2, 3, 4; *Das Altertum,* 19 (1973) 120–21, figs. 4–5, no. 6 (B); *LIMC,* II, pl. 531, Artemis 1096; Zimmermann, *Griechische Vasen,* pl. 8 (B).

219.73 VORONEZH, BM 157 (once Tartu, University, 99). *ABV* 478.4; *BAdd* 120.

220.74 NAPLES, 81111 (H 2537). *ABV* 477; *Para* 217.74; *CV* 1, pl. 41.2–3; *LIMC,* VIII, pl. 423, Kentauroi et Kentaurides 139 (A, B).

220.75 SÉVRES, 56. *ABV* 477.

220.76 LONDON, Leventis (once Northampton, Castle Ashby). *ABV* 477.1; *BAdd* 120.

220.77 LONDON, B 146. *ABV* 478.1.

220.78 NEW YORK, 21.88.92. *ABV* 478.7; *BAdd* 121.

220.79 NEW YORK, Gallatin. *ABV* 478.3; *Para* 217.

220.80 DETROIT, 63.10 (once San Simeon, 5599). *ABV* 478.1.

220.81 BEVERLEY HILLS, Prinzmetal (once San Simeon, 9520). *ABV* 478.2; *Para* 217.

220.82, 82 COLOGNY, Bodmer (once Basel, Market). *ABV* 478.8; *BAdd* 121; *LIMC,* IV, pl. 352, Helene 335 (B).

220.83 BERLIN, F 1881. *ABV* 478.2; *BAdd* 120; *Ausgestellte Werke,* 90, no. 2 (A); *LIMC,* V, pl. 222, Hermes 255 (A); Ronan, *Hekate,* 37, pl. 38B (drawing of A).

220.84 PALERMO. *ABV* 477.3.

220.85 BERLIN, F 1843. *ABV* 478; *Annali,* 8 (1986) fig. 60.2 (A); *Hephaistos,* 11/12 (1992/93) 73, fig. 19 (BD); Weber, *Badekultur,* 16, fig. 3 (A); Yegul, *Baths,* 19, fig. 19 (A).

220.86 SAN SIMEON, 10099 (S 483) (once Paris, market) ? *ABV* 481.1

220.87 LONDON, B 170. *ABV* 671.1; *BAdd* 148.

VASES RELATED TO THE EDINBURGH PAINTER

221.1 NEW HAVEN, 1913.111. Boardman, *ABFV,* fig. 240 (drawing); Brinkmann, *Beobachtungen,* 56, fig. a (drawing of part); Buitron, *New England,* 52, 53; Burke & Pollitt, 34–35, no.35.

221.2 SYRACUSE, 21154. *Ta Attika*, 283.F14 (parts).

221.3 CASTELVETRANO, 116. Lissarrague & Thelamon, 148, fig. 8 (drawing).

221.4 BOSTON, 95.15. *ABV* 480.

ADDENDA TO BEAZLEY'S ATTRIBUTIONS TO THE EDINBURGH
PAINTER

476.1 ATHENS, 19167. *Para* 217. Schnapp, *Chasseur*, 237, no. 158 (parts).

NAPLES, Museo di Capodimonte, 972. *Para* 218. Schnapp, *Chasseur*, 237, no.
156 (part).

476.2 TARANTO, 52232. *Taranto* I.3, 239, no. 45.1 (BD).

476.3 TARANTO, 52160. *Taranto* I.3, 57, 254, no. 60.2 (part, colour of part).

476.4 TARANTO, 52161. *Taranto* I.3, 254, no. 60.3 (parts of BD).

477.7 BASEL, Z 369 (once Roman Market). *BAdd* 120. *LIMC*, VII, pl. 345,
Polyxene 2 (part); *Para* 217.

(477.8TER), 700 LAON, 37.892. *BAdd* 120. *Para* 217. *Rivista*, 16 (1992)
Ghedini figs. 2–3. Schnapp, *Chasseur*, 246, no. 174 (parts of BD).

(477) GELA, 13. *Para* 217; *Ta Attika*, 283.F15 (parts of BD).

By the Edinburgh Painter or very near him

479.3 ROME, M 474. Manakidou, *Parastaseis*, pl. 31B (A).

479.4 LOS ANGELES, 50.8.19. *BAdd* 121;. *LIMC*, VI, pl. 12, Kerberos 16 (A).

Near the Edinburgh Painter

479.1 FRANKFURT, MusVF, β 342. Deppert, *Frankfurt*, 10 (A); *LIMC*, IV, pl.
131, Gigantes 244 (A); *Veder Greco*, 158–159, no. 38 (A, B).

479.5, 700 HAVANA, 149. Olmos, *Habana*, 119, no. 44 (A, B, AH).

Recalls the Edinburgh Painter

367.94 AGRIGENTO, 1531. *BAdd* 98; De Miro, *Templi*, pl. 37 (colour of A).

X. THE MARATHON PAINTER

92 ATHENS, 1040 (CC 836). *CV* 1, pl. 10 (18).7–8 (A, B); Petrakou, *Marathon*,
frontcover, 141, fig. 78 (C, Coulour of part of C).

93, 109, 132, 140 ATHENS, 1024 (CC 946). *ABV* 498.2; *CV* 1, pl. 10.5 (part); *Para* 233.

221.1, 90, 140, pl. 3.A–B (S, part of BD) ATHENS, 1011. Boardman, *ABFV*, fig. 256.

221.4 PALERMO, 1900 (79). *LIMC*, VI, pl. 194, Peleus 121 (part).

221.5 TOKYO, Eisei-Bunko, 2382 (once Paris, market). *CV*, Japan 2, pl. 64.3–5.

221.8 ATHENS, 1013. *CV* 1, pl. 11 (19).10.

221.9 ATHENS, 1014. *CV* 1, pl. 11 (19).8.

221.10 ATHENS, 1012. *CV* 1, pl. 11 (19).3.

222.11 ATHENS, 1015. *CV* 1, pl. 11 (19).6.

222.12 ATHENS, 1029. *CV* 1, pl. 11 (19).5.

222.14 ATHENS, 1016. *CV* 1, pl. 10 (18).16.

II. The group with much accessory decoration (thickset; lavish use of white ground)

222.17 READING, 45.X.6 (once London, Spink). *ABV* 487.

222.18, 89–90, 140, pl. 30.2A–C. ATHENS, 12273. Manakidou, *Parastaseis*, pl. 34.

222.19 SAN SIMEON, 12302 (once New York, Hearst). *ABV* 487.

222.22, pl. 30.1 (parts) SYRACUSE, 14569. *ABV* 487; *BAdd* 122; Boardman, *ABFV*, fig. 257; Brommer, *Heracles*, pl. 28; *LIMC*, V, pl. 81, Herakles 2416 (part); *Ta Attika*, 285.F19 (part of BD).

222.26 BRUSSELS, A 1311. *ABV* 488.3; Berard, *Images*, 91, fig. 4, 97, 99, pls. 1E, 3D (BD, drawings).

222.27 NEW YORK, 75.2.21 (GR 559). Berard, *Image* 97, pl. 1f, 100, pl. 4b (drawings); *Cité des Images*, 149, fig. 211; Pelling, *Tragedy*, pl. 4 (part).

222.28 PARIS, Market. *ABV* 488.2.

222.29 ATHENS, Vlasto. *ABV* 488.1.

222.31 LEIDEN, RO.II.20. Bastet, *Rottiers,* pl. 16.186 (part); *CV* 2, pl. 90.4–6.

III. Thickset as II (red-ground)

223.34 LONDON, B 560. *ABV* 495.158; *Para* 223; Hedreen, *Silens,* pl. 37 (part).

223.35 TARANTO, 6261. *ABV* 497; *CV* 1, pl. 14.3.5; *Taras, Rivista,* 10 (1990) 1, pl. 52

223.36, 91, pl. 31.1A–B MUNICH, 1874 (J 1113). *Kunst der Schale,* 421, fig. 75.11.

223.38 CATANIA, 665. *Para 222.*

223.39, 91, pl. 31.2 ATHENS, 1144. *Para 222.*

223.40 PARIS, ED 27. *Para 222.*

223.41 LONDON, B 558. *Para 222.*

223.43, 109 THEBES, 6136 (R80.236). *Para 222; CV,* pls. 64.4–6, 69.14.

LEKYTHOI CONNECTED WITH THE MARATHON PAINTER

Perhaps by his own hand:

223.1 ZURICH, 2476 (2331). *CV* I, pl. 17.10–13, 18, 19.

ADDENDA TO BEAZLEY'S ATTRIBUTIONS TO THE MARATHON
PAINTER

487.1 OXFORD, 1961.396. *Para 222; Ta Attika,* 285.F20 (parts of BD).

Near the Marathon Painter

488 LONDON, B 527. *LIMC,* V, pl. 131, Herakles 3017 (part).

Two vases by one hand:

223.2 NEW YORK, 08.258.29. *Para 225; BAdd* 123.

223.3 COPENHAGEN, B 76. *Para 225.*

Xbis. A CLASS OF LEKYTHOI NEAR THE MARATHON PAINTER

THE BEST BY THE PAINTER OF ATHENS 581, ALL RED-GOUND

(a) Some that are certainly by the painter of Athens 581

224.1, 93 ATHENS, 579. *ABV* 489.1.

224.3 PALERMO, 1949 (92). Sakowski *Dreifußkessel,* 396, fig. 39 (part).

224.4, 93, pl. 31.5 ATHENS, 581 (CC 915). *ABV* 492.84; *BAdd* 123; *Anz,* 1981,
323, fig. 6.

224.5 ATHENS, 383. *ABV* 491.62.

224.6 ATHENS, 396. *ABV* 492.80.

224.7 ATHENS, 578 (CC 928). *ABV* 493.100, 594; *Para* 223.

(β) Some published examples of the class of Athens 581

224.1 PARIS, CabMed, 282. *ABV* 489.13.

224.3 ATHENS, 1060. *ABV* 493.86.

224.4 PARIS, CabMed, 279. *ABV* 493.92.

224.5 CAMBRIDGE, GR 54.1864 (G 77). *ABV* 493.109; *BAdd* 123; *CV* 1, pl. 22.19.

224.6 CORINTH, MP 77. *ABV* 494.120; *Para* 223, 224; *BAdd* 123.

224.7 PARIS, F 362. *ABV* 494.132.

224.8 TORONTO, 920.68.73 (323). *ABV* 494.133; *BAdd* 123.

224.9 DELOS, 551. *ABV* 495.156.

224.10 PARIS, CabMed, 280. *ABV* 492.71; *BAdd* 122.

224.11 BELGRADE. *ABV* 490.39.

(γ) Some unpublished examples in Athens, from the workshop of the Painter of Athens 581

225.2 ATHENS, 394. *ABV* 492.77.

225.3 ATHENS, 385. *ABV* 492.85.

225.4 ATHENS, 388. *ABV* 493.107.

225.6 ATHENS, 384. *ABV* 493.108.

225.7 ATHENS, 12277. *ABV* 491.63.

(δ) Lekythoi of this class decorated with upright palmettes

225.1, 76, 93, 185, pl. 22.5 ATHENS, 12714. *ABV* 497.195; *Para* 242; *BAdd* 123.

225.6 NAPLES, 81036 (H 2785). *ABV* 497.196.

ADDENDA TO BEAZLEY'S ATTRIBUTIONS TO THE CLASS OF ATHENS A 581

The Class of Athens 581. i

488 LONDON, B 527. *LIMC*, V, pl. 131, Herakles 3017 (part).

491.44 TARANTO, 52208. *Taranto* I.3, 247, no. 53.4 (BD).

491.46 MELBOURNE, 1931.0003 (V 15). Connor & Jackson, *Melbourne*, 106–108, no. 37 (colour of BD, profile).

491.49 NEW YORK, Christie's (once Rossie Priory, Lord Kinnaird). *Christie's New York*, 4.6.1999, 13, no.15 (colour of part); *Sotheby's*, 10.12.1996, 64, no.117 right (part).

491.60 ADOLPHSECK, 12. *Para* 223; *BAdd* 122; *LIMC*, IV, pl. 101, Geras 3 (part).

491.64 BARCELONA, 377. *BAdd* 122; Trias de Arribas, pl. 26.1; *Arte Griego*, 200, fig. 258 (part).

492.70 OXFORD, 1934.249. *Para* 223; *BAdd* 122; *LIMC*, VIII, pl. 672, Polyphemos I 46.

492.73 KARLSRUHE 171 (B 2). *Para* 223; *Veder Greco*, 152, no. 34.

(492.75BIS) 716 ATHENS, Agora, P 24109. *Para* 223; *BAdd* 122; *LIMC*, VI, pl. 567, NIKE 89 (part).

(492.85BIS) 716 ATHENS, Agora, P 24060. *BAdd* 124; *Hesperia*, 62 (1993) pl. 81C (part).

493.95 BARCELONA, 375. *BAdd* 123; *REA* 88 (1986) 375, fig. 54C (part).

(493.97TER) 716 ATHENS, Agora, P 24055. *BAdd* 123; *Hesperia*, 55 (1986) pl. 11, no. 112; *Hesperia*, 62 (1993) pl. 81.A (part).

493.102 LONDON, Sotheby's (once Rossie Priory, Lord Kinnaird). *Sotheby's*, 10.12.1996, no. 117 left (part).

494.121 THEBES, 6140 (R.80.237). *CV*, pls. 65.4–6, 69.16.

496.163 THEBES, 6145 (R.80.241). *CV*, pls. 64.1–3, 69.13.

496.165 GERONA, 817. *BAdd* 123; *Arte Griego*, 170, fig. 219; *REA*, 88 (1986) 374, fig. 53B (part).

496.166 BONN, 1555. *BAdd* 128; *LIMC*, IV, pl. 542, Herakles 1472.

(496.166BIS) 701 PRAGUE, 2475, 2477. *Para* 223; *CV*, 1, 67, fig. 40.1, pl. 41.1–3.

496.167 LONDON B 549. *LIMC*, V, pl. 221, Hermes 252.

496.183 NEW YORK, Sotheby's (once Boston, 81.171 (R 338)). *Sotheby-Parke-Bernet*, 2.6.2001, 156–157, no. 259.

496.184 LONDON, Christie's (once Nostel Priory, Lord St. Oswald, 37). *Para* 223; *BAdd* 123; *Christie's*, 25.4.2001, 239, no.541 (colour of part).

497.187 CORINTH, C 47.162. *Hesperia*, 64 (1995) pl. 72.180 (part).

497 TARANTO, 50287. *Taranto* I.3, 95, 239, no. 46.1 (BD, colour of part); Lippolis, *Eroi*, 33–34, figs. 24–25 (parts).

(497.196BIS) 716 ATHENS, Agora, P 24119. *Para* 242; *BAdd* 123; *Hesperia*, 62 (1993) pl. 82L.1 (part).

(497) GLASGOW, Burrell, 19.12. *CV*, pl. 23.9–11.

(**497**) AVIGNON, S 63. *Para* 224; Cavalier, *Silence et Fureur*, 193, fig. 74.

(**497**) GELA, 97. *Para* 224; *Ta Attika*, 285.F21 (part of BD).

(**497**) GELA, 96. *Para* 225; *Ta Attika*, 286.F22 (parts of BD).

(**497**) GELA, 8724. *Para* 225; *Ta Attika*, 286.F23 (parts of BD).

(**497**) ST. PETERSBURG, 1912.9. *Para* 225; *TrudyErm*, 28 (1997) 29, fig. 8 (part).

(**497**) ATHENS, Agora, P 24472. *Para* 228, 281; *BAdd* 123; Carpenter, *Fifth-Century Imagery*, pl. 39A (part).

(**497**) GELA, N 42. *Para* 228; *Ta Attika*, 286.F24 (parts of BD); *CV,* 4, pl. 24.1, 4.7–8.

(**497**) TARANTO, 52256. *Para* 228; *Taranto* I.3, 285, no. 77.1 (part).

(**497**) AGRIGENTO, C 832. *CV,* 1, pls. 61.3–4, 63.2; *Para* 225.

Class of Athens 581. ii

(**498.1TER**) 701 PRAGUE, 781. *Para* 231; *CV,* 1, 69, fig. 41.1, pl. 42.78; *LIMC*, IV, pl. 132, Gigantes 254 S.

498.4 OLYMPIA, K 10798. *Olympische Forschungen*, 28 (2000) pl. 78.175 (BD).

499.29 THEBES, 6138 (R.80.245). *CV,* pls. 66.4–6, 69.18.

(**499.32BIS**) 702 SORRENTO, 117. Sakowski, *Dreifußkessel*, 398–399, figs. 41–42 (parts).

499.34 BERLIN (once Mainz, Brommer). *BAdd* 124; Grabow, *Schlangenbilder*, pl. 18.K86 (part).

500.51 ATHENS, 489 (CC 882). *BAdd* 124; *LIMC*, I, 455, Aktaion 1 (drawing), pl. 346, Aktaion 2; Marconi, *Selinunte,* 260, fig. 118 (drawing).

501.72 GLASGOW, Hunterian Museum, D 87. *CV,* pl. 23.15–16.

501.81 TARANTO, 50288. *Taranto* I.3, 239, no. 46.2 (part).

501.87 TARANTO, 50289. *Taranto* I.3, 239, no. 46.3 (part).

502.97 LYONS, Metzger. *BAdd* 124; *Archeologia Classica*, 50 (1998) 348, fig. 6 (part of BD).

502.118 GENEVA, F 162. *BAdd* 124; Birchler Emery, Musique, pls. 14, 16.61 (parts).

(**503**) GELA, 17. *Para* 234, 240; *Ta Attika*, 287.F25 (parts of BD).

(**503**) STAVANGER, 4303. *Para* 236; *LIMC*, IV, pl. 132, Gigantes 254 T (parts).

(**503**) GELA, 5. *Para* 236; *CV,* 4, pls. 22.4–6, 23.3–4; *Ta Attika*, 287.F26 (part).

(503) ATHENS, Agora, P 24330. *Para* 238, 237; *BAdd* 125; *LIMC*, IV, pl. 138, Gigantes 293.

(503) GELA, 66. *Para* 241; *Ta Attika*, 288.F28 (parts of BD).

The Kalinderu Group

504.18 ELEUSIS, 2409. Pelling, *Tragedy*, pls. 6A–B (parts).

Palmette-lekythoi of style (a)

ATHENS, Agora, P 24531. *Para* 242; *Hesperia*, 62 (1993) pl. 82L.3 (part).

ATHENS, Agora, P 16770. *Para* 243; *Hesperia*, 62 (1993) pl. 82K.3 (part).

ATHENS, Agora, P 24527. *Para* 243; *Hesperia*, 62 (1993) pl. 82M.2 (part).

ATHENS, Agora, P 24528. *Para* 243; *Hesperia*, 62 (1993) pl. 82M.3 (part).

ATHENS, Agora, P 24529. *Para* 243; *Hesperia*, 62 (1993) pl. 82M.4 (part).

ATHENS, Agora, P 24526. *Para* 243; *Hesperia*, 62 (1993) pl. 82M.1 (part).

ATHENS, Agora, P 24530. *Para* 243; *Hesperia*, 62 (1992) pl. 82L.2 (part).

ATHENS, Agora, P 1382. *Para* 243; *Hesperia*, 62 (1993) pl. 82K2 (part).

XI. THE SAPPHO PAINTER

Lekythoi

(a) Black-figure, of normal shape

225.1 COPENHAGEN, B 87 (VIII 390). *CV* 3, pl. 111.1; Cesare, *Statue in Immagine*, 213, fig. 149 (parts).

225.2 NEW YORK, 06.1021.70. *ABV* 507.2.

225.3 NEW YORK, 41.162.35. *ABV* 507.3.

225.4 OXFORD, 1934.248. Lissarrague, *Céramique*, 185–186, figs. 1B, 3A–B (parts of BD, profile).

225.5 NEW YORK, 41.162.34. *ABV* 507.5, 702; *BAdd* 126; Immerwahr, *Attic Script* pl. 25.106 (part); Mertens, *White Ground*, pl. 36.1 (where the museum number is incorrect).

226.6, 96, 98–99, 113, 120.3, pl. 32.1A–D NEW YORK, 41.162.29 (once New York, Gallatin). *ABV* 507.6, 702; *BAdd* 126; Buitron-Oliver, *New Perspectives*, 50, fig. 18 (drawing); *Classical Antiquity*, 12 (1993) fig. 8 at p. 266 (part); *LIMC*,

IV, pls. 80, Ganymedes 59, 122, Gigantes 144 (parts); *LIMC*, V, pl. 638, Helios 105; *Looking at Greek Vases*, 109, fig. 44 (drawing).

226.7 PARIS, MNB 910. *AK*, 28 (1985) pl. 38.3; *Potters and Painters* 285, fig. 1; Lissarrague, *Céramique*, 185, fig. 1D (profile); *LIMC*, II, pl. 241, Apollon 701A.

226.8, 96, 98,123, pls. 33.1A–C, 35.2 ATHENS, 595 (CC 968). Aktseli, *Altäre*, pl. 1.2 (part); Lissarrague, *Céramique*, 185, fig. 1E (profile); *LIMC*, VII, pl. 220, Pelops 12 (parts); Lacroix, *Etudes*, pl. 14; *Nikephoros*, 4 (1991) 319, figs. 1A–B (parts); van Straten, *Hiera Kala*, fig. 153 (part).

226.9 ROME, 50561 (M 570). *AJA*, 84 (1980) pl. 38, fig. 2 (part); Lissarrague, *Céramique*, 186, fig. 4 (drawing of BD); *LIMC*, VII, pl. 707, Kyknos I 120 (parts); Mingazzini, P., *Vasi della Collezione Castellani*, I (Rome, 1930) pls. 86.6, 87.1–3.

226.10, pl. 35.1 (part) NEW YORK, 41.162.30. *ABV* 507.10.

226.11, pl. 33.2 PARIS, CA 156 (L 26). Lissarrague, *Céramique*, 185, fig. 1 (profile); *LIMC*, VII, pl. 198, Peleus 165 (part); Verbanck-Pierard, *Hippocrate*, 269 (part).

226.12 KARLSRUHE, 184. *ABV* 507.12; *LIMC*, VI, pl. 489, Nereides 257 (part).

226.13 PARIS, CabMéd. *Fest Hampe*, 317, fig. 5 (drawing); Stähler, *Patroklos*, fig. 11 (drawing).

226.16 LONDON, Winslow (once London, Market, Spink). *ABV* 507.16.

226.18 NAPLES, 111609. Herrmann, *Omphalos*,41, fig. 3 (drawing); *LIMC*, III, pl. 548, Elektra 54; Prag, *Oresteia* (Warminster, 1985) pl. 33 b–c (drawing).

226.21 PALERMO, NI 1107. Recke, *Gewalt*, pl.47c.

226.23 LONDON, B 544. *LIMC*, V, pl. 232, Hermes 425C (part).

226.26 AGRIGENTO, C 847. *CV* 1, pl. 71.1–2.

(β) Black-figure, of little-lion shape

On the shoulder, lotus-buds:

227.28, pl. 36.1 (part) LONDON, B 639. Boardman, *ABFV*, fig. 261; *LIMC*, VI, pl. 11, Ker 58 (part) pls. 233–234, Memnon 18; Vermeule, *Aspects,* 161, fig. 14; Lissarrague, *Céramique,* 185, fig. 1F (profile).

227.29 LONDON, B 526. *LIMC*, IV, pl. 127, Gigantes 201 (part).

227.32 LONDON, 1910.2–12.1. *ABV* 507.32; *BAdd* 126; *LIMC*, VIII, pl. 569, Midas 10 (part); Lissarrague, *Banquet,*15, fig. 4 (drawing of BD); Lissarrague, *Guerrier* 120, fig. 67 (drawing); *Meddelelser,* 47 (1991) 15, fig. 9 (drawing of BD); Settis, *Greci,*1282, fig. 1 (part).

227.35 BASEL, BS 1921.358. *CV* I, pl. 54.2–3; *LIMC*, IV, pl. 133, Gigantes 256 d (part).

227.36 BASEL, BS 1921.357. *CV* I, pl. 54.1,4.

On the shoulder, two lions, confronted:

227.37, 98–99, 139, pl. 35.3a–d ATHENS, 552. Boardman, *ABFV*, fig. 262.1, 2.

227.38 SYRACUSE, 20936. Meyer, *Medeia*, pl. 16.1 (drawing); *Ta Attika*, 288.F29 (part); Halm-Tisserant, *Cannibalisme*, pl. 3, fig. 8 (drawing).

227.39, 99 GELA, 40224 (N 30) (once Gela, Navarra). *Para* 246; *CV*, 3, pls. 21.3–4, 22.3–4; *Ta Attika*, 288.F30 (parts of BD).

227.40 PROVIDENCE, 14.432 (C 2155). Krieger, *Peleus und Thetis*, pl. 5B.

(γ) Black-figure lekythoi that are probably his, judging from the publications

227.40*bis* LONDON, 2000.11–16.1 (Colossus 2) (once Naples, Hamilton). *CV* 10, 44–45, pls. A.16, 15.16.

227.40*ter* UNKNOWN. LIMC, IV, 493, Hektor 89 (drawing).

(δ) In Six's technique, of normal shape

227.41 NAPLES, 86382 (RC 185). *CV* 5, pls. 66.1–3, 74.6, fig. 15; Moraw, *Mänade*, pl. 8.24 (BD).

228.48 SYRACUSE, 26822. Beck, *Album*, pl. 85.412; *LIMC*, II, pl. 697, Atalante 70. *Nikephoros*, 3 (1990) 323, fig. 12 (part).

228.49 NAPLES, 86339 (RC 172). *CV* 5, pl. 67, fig. 16; *LIMC*, I, pl. 322, Aithiopes 5; Snowden, *Blacks*, 50, fig. 21.

228.50BIS BRUSSELS, van Branteghem. *ABV* 675.

228.53, 81, 95, 104–106, pls. 34.2A–B, 36.2 ATHENS, 2184. *ABV* 481A; Boardman, *ABFV*, fig. 263; Duby and Perrot, *Femmes*, 247, fig. 61 (A).

228.54, 54, 81, 104, 106, pl. 34.1A–C ELEUSIS, 907. *BCH*, 108 (1984) 100–102, figs. 1–3; Berti and Restani, *musica*, 36, fig. 7 (parts).

228.54bis MALIBU, 91.AE.22 (once Adria, Bocchi). *CV* 2, pl. 73.3.

228.56, 94, 96, 106, 113, 115 WARSAW, 142333 (once Goluchow, Czartorski, 32). Boardman, *ABFV*, fig. 311 (part); *Naked Truths*, 110, fig. 13 (part); Santi, *Collezioni*, Dobrowolski fig. 13 (part of BD).

228.57, 113, 115 KARLSRUHE, B 32 (167). *ABV* 507.57; *BAdd* 126; *CV* I, pl. 9.1–3 (A, B); Ebertshäuser & Waltz, 99, fig. 116 (A); *150 Jahre Antikensammlungen*, 43, fig. 28 (A); Kurtz, *AWL*, pl. 55.1 (part of A); *LIMC*, VI, pl. 628, Odysseus 105 (A); Mertens, *White Ground*, pl. 11.1 (side); Andreae,

Ulisse, 131–132, figs. 2.22–23 (A, colour of A); Vogt, *Griechische Literatur,* 42 (A); Buitron, *Odyssey,* 35, fig. 18..

229.58 PARIS, MNB 905 (L 4). *AJA,* 95 (1991) 630, fig. 1; *Anz,* 1977, 596, fig. 21; Arrigoni, *Donne,*226, pl. 7; Boardman, *ABFV,* fig. 265; *Archaic Greek Art,* 311, fig. 356; Delavaud-Roux, *Danses Armées,* 126, no.54 (drawing of part); Duby and Perrot, *Femmes,* 187, fig. 14 (drawing); Kurtz and Boardman, *Burial Customs,* pl. 33; Mommsen, *Exekias* I, Beilage C; Pfisterer-Haas, *Alte Frauen,* 177, fig. 26; Rühfel, *Kind,* 41, fig. 14; Scheibler, *Malerei,* 131, fig. 59; Kurtz and Boardman, *Thanatos,* 171, fig. 50; Fantham, *Women,* 48, fig. 1.13; Boardman, *History,* 229, fig. 250.

115, **229.59** ATHENS, 450 (CC 688). *ADelt,* 24.1 (1969) pl. 125; *AJA,* 95 (1991) 640, figs. 12–13 (A); *AM,* 16 (1891) 379 (drawing of part); Baumeister, *Denkmäler,* I, 306, fig. 321, III, 1975, fig. 2114 (drawings of A, B); Boardman, *ABFV,* fig. 264.1, 2 (B); Brijder, *Proceedings,* 319, fig. 4A–B (NA, part of B); *CV* I, pls. 8 (16).1–2, 9 (17).3; Cook, *Zeus,* 1056, fig. 912; *Jb,* 100 (1985) 44, fig. 10D (part of A); Kurtz & Boardman, *Burial Customs,* pl. 36 (NA, B); *LIMC,* VIII, 568, Eidola 12 (drawing of NA); *Mind and Body,* 144–145, no. 34 (A, part); Peifer, *Eidola,* pl. 6.13, no. 76 (drawing); Kurtz, and Boardman, *Thanatos,* 181 & 183, figs. 55A–B (parts); Vermeule, *Aspects,* 21, fig. 17 (B).

LEKYTHOI NEAR THE SAPPHO PAINTER

229.1 NEW YORK, 41.162.138 (once Gallatin). *ABV* 702.

229.2 LYONS, 75. *ABV* 508.2, 677.

XIbis. GROUPS OF LEKYTHOI BY COMPANIONS OF THE SAPPHO

PAINTER AND THE DIOSPHOS PAINTER

229.3, 116–117 NEW YORK, Sotheby's (once Munich, Market). Heesen, *Theodor,* 21, pl. 15, 88, 90, no. 15 (including colour of part and profile); *MededAPM,* 66–67 (1996) 17, pl. 2B, 32, fig. 18 (colour of part, parts); *SothPB,* 17.12.1998, 24, no. 72 (part, colour of part); Boardman, *History,* 201, fig. 218.1–2 (parts).

Near these three

229, 117 TÜBINGEN, S/10.1294 (D 68) (once Munich, Arndt). *CV* 3, pl. 47.1–4; *LIMC,* VII, pl. 127, Paridis iudicium 108.

Three white-ground lekythoi, of little-lion shape,

By one hand (The Kephisophon Painter)

230.1, 117.1 NEW YORK, 08.258.30. *ABV* 514, 669; *BAdd* 148; Sweet, *Sport*, 50, pl. 14 (part).

230.2, pl. 40.4A–B BOSTON, 98.922. *Hesperia*, 43 (1974) pl. 90B (part).

230.3, 117.3 UNKNOWN (once New York, Gallatin). *ABV* 514, 669, *BAdd* 148.

The 'hound-and-hare group'

230.1, 118 LONDON, V&A, C 2490.1912. *ABV* 514.

230.3, 118.2 MUNICH, 1864. *ABV* 514.

230.4, 118.3 TÜBINGEN, S.10/1291 (D 67) (once Munich, Arndt). *CV* 3, pls. 39.1, 2, 40.5.

230.6 UNKNOWN (once Coghill). *ABV* 514.

230.11 PARIS, F 190. *ABV* 516.7.

231.14 MUNICH, 1863. *ABV* 514.

231.15 MUNICH, 1865 (J 1266). *ABV* 516.1; Schnapp, *Chasseur*, 262, no. 217 (part of S).

The 'krotala group' of little-lion shape; some examples

231.1, 119.1 AGRIGENTO, C 780. *CV* 1, pl. 73.1–2.

231.2, 119.2 NEW YORK, 1906.1021.158. *LIMC*, VII, pl. 194, Peleus 126 (part).

231.5 BERLIN, F 1997. *ABV* 515.

231.7, 119 PARIS,CA 1730. Christiansen and Melander, *Proceedings*, 339, fig. 2A–C; *Fest Thimme*, 66, fig. 6 (part); *LIMC*, VIII, pl. 756, Silenoi 59.

XII. THE DIOSPHOS PAINTER

232.1 TARANTO, 4416. *Taranto* I.3, 325, no. 107.1 (BD).

232.4 LECCE, 565. *CV* 1, pl. 4 (151).5–7; Lissarrague, *Guerrier* 57, fig. 25 (B).

232.6 VATICAN, 450 (10). *ABV* 508.6.

232.9, 95 CORINTH, C 33.130. *Hesperia*, 64 (1995) pl. 74.190.

232.10 SYRACUSE, 19901. *Ta Attika*, 289.F31 (parts).

232.14 BRUSSELS, R 326. *CV* 2, pl. 1 (62).1; Vanhove, *deporte* 387, no.257 (colour of part); Vanhove, *Sport* 387, no.257 (colour of part).

233.15 NEW YORK, 25.70.2. Stähler, *Patroklos*, fig. 5 (drawing).

233.16 ATHENS, Market. *ABV* 668.

233.18, pl. 36.4a–b AGRIGENTO, C 846 (once Politi). *CV* I, pls. 71.3–4, 72.3.

233.19 PARIS, CA 598. *Archeo*, 107 (January 1994) 65 (colour of part); Boardman, *ABFV*, fig. 270 (drawing); *LIMC*, V, pl. 54, Herakles 2004 (part); *QuadTic*, 25 (1996) 45, pl. 3.8 (part); *Hommes, Dieux et Héros*, 224–25, figs. 91A–D; Lissarrague, *Céramique*,185, fig. 2B (profile); Lissarrague, *Greek Vases*, 124–125 (drawing, colour of part).

233.20 CAMBRIDGE (MA), 1925.30.49. *CV*, Hoppin & Gallatin, pl. 19 (19).1, 3; *LIMC*, III, pl. 188, Cheiron 23; *Centaur's Smile*, no. 39.

233.31 PARIS, CA 601. *LIMC*, III, pl. 55, Automedon 21 (part); *QuadTic*, 23 (1994) 42, fig. 6 (part). Stähler, *Patroklos*, fig. 6 (drawing).

233.36, 100, 110, pl. 36.5 ATHENS, 2213. Lissarrague, *Céramique*,185, fig. 2E (profile).

233.39 BERLIN, F 2003. *LIMC*, VII, pl. 198, Peleus 167 (part).

234.49 KARLSRUHE, B 1512 (B 187). *ABV* 508.49; *CV* I, pl. 13.5–6.

234.51 ATHENS, E 1167 (once Empedokles). *ABV* 508.51.

234.52 COPENHAGEN, B 96 (VIII.946). *CV* 3, pl. 112.2; *LIMC*, V, pl. 460, Iolaos 22 (part).

234.53 OXFORD, 1935.42. *ABV* 508.53; Lissarrague, *Céramique*, 185, fig. 2F (profile).

234.55 HEIDELBERG, L 60. *CV* 4, pl. 171.5, 6.

234.56 COPENHAGEN, 1677. *CV* 3, pl. 111.5.

234.60 CAMBRIDGE, GR 101.1864 (G 126). *CV* I, pl. 22.29.

234.61 CORINTH, T 1081. *Para* 275; *Hesperia*, 64 (1995) pl. 92.4 (part).

235.62 CORINTH, T 1325. *Hesperia*, 64 (1995) pl. 92.5 (part).

Lekythoi with two-figure groups between palmettes, and 'semi-outline'

235.66, 94, 97, 110, 124–127, 130, pl. 37.2 ATHENS, 12271 (N 943). Kurtz, *AWL*, pl. 69.1.

235.67 UNIVERSITY, 77.3.82 (once Baltimore, Robinson). *CV*, Robinson I, pl. 38.7A–C; Shapiro, *Southern Collections*, 25, no. 5.

235.69 BOSTON, 99.528. *ARV*² 301.2, 303.1, 1643; *BAdd* 211.

235.70, 111, pl. 39.1 (part) PARIS, MNB 909 (L 31). *ARV*² 301.4, 303.3; *ABV* 508.70; *BAdd* 212; Rumpf, *MuZ*, pl. 21.1; Lissarrague, *Céramique*, 185, fig. 2A (profile).

235.71 NEW YORK, 06.1070. *ARV*² 301.3, 303.2, 1643; *BAdd* 212; Immerwahr, *Attic Script* pl. 25.108 (part); *Ktema*, 11 (1986) pl. 4.7 (drawing of part); Mertens,

White Ground, pl. 36.3 (BD); Robertson, *Vase-Painting*, 131, fig. 134 (part); *LIMC*, IV, pl. 184, Gorgo, Gorgones 309; Schefold, *Urkönige*, 102, fig. 123.

(β) In Six's technique,

Of normal shape and size, in his bold style

235.72 TARANTO, 4571 (31). *Taranto* I.3, 250–251, no. 56.1 (BD).

235.74 LONDON, B 688. *Para* 248.

235.76, pls. 37.3, 38.4 PARIS, MNB 912. *LIMC*, I, pl. 394, Alexandros 92 (A); *LIMC*, V, pl. 485, Iris I 16; Lonis, *Guerre*, fig. 11.

235.78 KARLSRUHE, 231. *Para* 248.

236.81, pl. 38.6 (part) BOSTON, 98.885. *Para* 248; *Ta Attika*, 289.F32 (part of BD).

236.86 PARIS, MNB 2861. Lissarrague, *Céramique,* 185, fig. 2C (profile); *LIMC*, VI, pl. 238, Memnon 73.

236.87 AGRIGENTO, C 729. *CV* 1, pl. 85.4.

236.90 BERLIN, F 2241. *ABV* 508.90.

236.91 LONDON, 37.6–9.72 (B 687). *LIMC*, VI, pl. 628, Odysseus 106; Touchefeu-Meynier, *Thèmes Odysséens*, pl. 11.3; Andreae, *Ulisse*, 50, fig. 9 (colour of part); Wijer, *Polyphemusavontuur*, fig. 131; Lissarrague, *Céramique*, 185, fig. 2D (profile).

236.92 NEW YORK, 1924.97.29. *LIMC*, VI, pl. 238, Memnon 70; *MetMusJ*, 22 (1987) 11, fig. 7 (part); Recke, *Gewalt*, pl. 45b.

236.93 PARIS, CabMéd, 493 (once Paris, Duke of Luynes, once Durand). *CV* 2, pl. 95.2, 5, 10.

236.96 PARIS, CabMéd, 492 (once Oppermann, 29). *CV* 2, pl. 95.1, 3, 4.

236.101, 100, 107 ATHENS, 14654. *ABV* 510.19.

237.103, 113 AMSTERDAM, 318. *CV*, Scheurleer 1, pl. 1 (37).1.

237.108, pl. 37.1A–B BERLIN, F 2032. Schefold, *Göttersage*, 211, figs. 289–90.

237.109, pl. 37.4A–D PARIS, CA 1706. *LIMC*, II, pl. 253, Apollon 781D.

237.111, pl. 38.1 (part) OXFORD, 1919.35. Boardman, *ABFV*, fig. 268 (part).

237.112 PARIS, MusRodin, 533. *ABV* 509.112; *CV*, pls. 20.3, 6–9.

237.114 NAPLES, 86387 (RC 209). *CV* 5, pls. 69.1, 75.3.

237.115 UNKNOWN (once Barcelona, Montaner). *ABV* 509.115; Mertens, *White Ground*, pl. 14.1 (part).

237.117 GERONA, 9. Mertens, *White Ground*, pl. 14.2; Trias de Arribas pl. 39.1.

237.117BIS GERONA, 826. Trias de Arribas pl. 39.2.

237.118 PARIS, MNC 624. *ABV* 481b; *Archeo*, 158, April 1998, 74–75 (colour of A); *LIMC*, I, pl. 520, Amazones 752 B (A); *REA*, 94 (1992) 348, fig. 1 (B).

238.120 PARIS, CabMed, 219. *ABV* 509.120; *BdA*, 36 (1951) 8, fig. 9 (A); *LIMC*, IV, pl. 424, Hera 322 (A); *AM*, 112 (1997) pl. 18.1 (B).

238.121 BERLIN, F 1837. *ABV* 509.121, 703; *Para* 248; *Ausgestellte Werke*, 102, no. 2 (B); *Classical Antiquity*, 15 (1996) fig. 21 at p.77 (B); *Nikephoros*, 3 (1990) 323, fig. 11 (B); Sweet, *Sport*, 135, pl. 45 (A).

238.122, 120.6 PARIS, CabMéd, 220. *Para* 248; *LIMC*. V, pl. 638 Helios 103 (A).

238.123 WARSAW, 142328 (once Goluchow, Czartorski, 15). Beck, *Album*, pl. 1.2 (A); *CV* Goluchow 1, pl. 12.3A–B; Santi, *Collezioni*, Dobrowolski, fig. 8 (A).

238.124 WARSAW, 142326 (once Goluchow, Czartorski, 12). Santi, *Collezioni*, Dobrowolski fig. 9 (A).

238.129 OXFORD, 217. *Para* 248.129.

238.130 PARIS, F 385.*ABV* 509.130; *LIMC*, VII, pl. 687, Kyknos I 9 (A).

238.131 PARIS, F 386. *Anz*, 1971, 172, figs. 17–18 (A, B); *LIMC*, V, pl. 54, Herakles 2003 (A)

238.132 PARIS, F 387. Flaceliere and Devambez, pl. 7 (A, B); *Hommes, Dieux et Héros*, 222–23, fig. 90a–b (A, B).

238.133 PARIS, F 388. Hyatt, *Vase*, figs. 76–77 (A, B); *LIMC*, VII, pl. 521, Sarpedon 7 (A); *MiscManni*, VI, pl. 2 at 1944 (A); Shapiro, *Personifications*, 136, fig. 89 (A); Recke, *Gewalt*, pl. 43b.

239.135 PARIS, F 384 BIS (CA 1961). *LIMC*, IV, pl. 240, Harmonia 9 (A); *Para* 248.135; Schefold and Jung, *Urkönige,*37, fig. 27 (part); Cavalier, *Silence et Fureur,* 435, fig. 130 (colour of A); *LIMC* V, pl. 562, Kadmos I 45 (A); Onians, *Classical Art*, 35, fig.26 (A); Lissarrague, *Greek Vases*, 130, fig. 103 (colour of BD).

239.136 UNIVERSITY, 77.3.58 (once Oxford, Robinson). *Para* 248.136; *GVGetty* 6 (2000) 52, fig. 4 (A); Shapiro, *Sothern Collections*, 49, no. 16.

239.137 NEW YORK, 56.171.25 (once San Simeon, 9846). *ABV* 509.137; *Para* 248; *BAdd* 127; *LIMC*, VI, pl. 237, Memnon 63 (A); *LIMC*, VII, pl. 521, Sarpedon 8 (A); Peifer, *Eidola,* pl. 8, fig. 17 (drawing of A); Shapiro, *Personifications*, 137, fig. 90 (A); Boardman, *History*, 65, fig. 86 (A); Recke, *Gewalt*, pl. 45a.

239.138 NEW YORK, X 21.15 (GR 523). *CV* 4, pl. 50.1, 2; *LIMC*, V, pl. 490, Iris I 70 (A); Richter& Milne, fig. 17 (B).

239.139 PHILADELPHIA, 64.177 (once Memorial Hall, 99.169). *ABV* 509.139; *Expedition*, 36 (1994) 2–3, A27 (A).

239.140 VIENNA, 668. *ABV* 509.140.

239.141 ST. PETERSBURG, 1466 (ST 59). Gorbunova, *Chernofigurnie*, 145, no. 114 (A, B); *LIMC*, VII, pl. 712, Kyknos I 142 (A).

239.142 HAMBURG, 1927.143 (89). *Anz*, 1928, 311–2, figs. 33–4 (A, B).

239.143 ST. PETERSBURG, 1463 (288). *Para* 248.143; *BAdd* 127.

239.144 ST. PETERSBURG, 1302 (B 289, ST 65). Gorbunova, *Chernofigurnie*, 144, no. 113 (A, B); *TrudyErm* 28 (Sankt Petersburg, 1997) 111, fig. 5 (A).

240.145 ST. PETERSBURG, 1462 (B 287, ST 74). Gorbunova, *Chernofigurnie*, 147, no.116 (A, B).

240.146 MOSCOW, II1B78. *CV* 1, pl. 13 (A, B); Sidorova, *Pushkin Museum*, 15, pls. 61–62, no. 32.

240.147 MOSCOW, II 1B 77. *Para* 248.147; *CV* 1, pl. 12 (A, B); Sidorova, *Pushkin Museum*, 15, pls. 59–60, no. 31.

240.148 VIENNA, 3599. *LIMC*, 3, pl. 187, Cheiron 21 (B).

240.149 ROME, MusBarracco, 223. *Para* 269; *Gymnasium*, 77 (1970) pls. 1, 2 (A, B); *LIMC*, pl. 548, Nessos 82.

240.150 NEW YORK, 41.162.175. *ABV* 509.150.

240.151 NORMAN, C 45.46.5 (once Paris, market, Hirsch). *ABV* 509.151; Heisserer, *Stovall Museum*, pl. at 76, no.85 (A, B).

240.152 CAPUA, 7555 (446). *ABV* 703.152; *CV*, pl. 4.5–6 (A, B).

240.153 FLORENCE. Brommer, *Herakles* II, pl. 7B (A); *LIMC*, VI, pl. 16, Kerkopes 6.

240.154 CAPUA, 7557. *ABV* 703.154; *CV*, pl. 5.1–2 (A, B).

240.155 NEW YORK, 41.162.178. *ABV* 509.155; *CV* Gallatin, pl. 39.2; *LIMC*, IV, pl. 222, Hades 147 (A).

240.156 NEW YORK, 56.171.26 (once San Simeon, 9484). *ABV* 509.156; *LIMC*, VI, pl. 58, Kreousa III 30.

240.158 BASEL, BS 1906.265. *ABV* 482.8; *Para* 248.158.

240.159 NAPLES, 81099 (H 3359, M 910). *LIMC*, IV, pl. 558, Herakles 1674.

240.160, pl. 39.2 (part of A) PARIS, MN 42 (F 234) (N 3211). Ahlberg-Cornell, *Herakles* 152, no. XI 6 (A, B); *CV* 4, pl. 45 (211) 2, 4, 5, 7; Ghiron-Bistagne, *Recherches,* 292, figs. 150, 151 (erroneous attribution); *LIMC*, VI, pl. 533, Nereus 122 (B).

241.161 MUNICH, 1582 (J 1155). *LIMC*, VII, pl. 195, Peleus 135 (A).

ADDENDA TO BEAZLEY'S ATTRIBUTIONS TO THE SAPPHO AND
DIOSPHOS PAINTERS

498 GLASGOW, Burrell, 19.12. *CV*, pl. 23.9–11.

508 MADRID, 10916 (L 65). *BICS*, 37 (1990) pl. 7A (part of B); Carpenter, *Art
and Myth*, fig. 222 (B); *LIMC*, IV, pl. 544, Herakles 1502 (A); *LIMC*, V, pl. 465,
Iole I2, 483, Iphitos I3 (B); Pochmarski, *Dionysische Gruppen*, pl. 1.1 (drawing
of A); *Rivista*, 19 (1995) fig. 3 (B); Wolf, *Herakles*, figs. 32–33 (A).

508.1 GÖTTINGEN, J 22. *BAdd* 127; *Nikephoros*, 4 (1991) 320, fig. 2 (parts);
Shapiro, *Myth into Art*, 81, figs. 52–54.

510.21 NEW YORK, Sotheby's (once Bastis). *Para* 249; *BAdd* 128; Bothmer,
Bastis, 269, no. 157 (parts); *SothPB*, 9.12.1999, 154, no. 134 (colour of parts).

517.1 PARIS, MARKET. *Para* 250, *BAdd* 128, *Centaur's Smile*, 67, no. 24;
Callipolitis-Feytmans, pl. 54 bottom.

BRUNSWICK, 1984.23. *Para* 247; *BAdd* 126; *AJA*, 95 (1991) 634, fig. 4 (A);
Kurtz and Boardman, *Burial Customs*, figs. 37, 38, 39; Kurtz and Boardman,
Thanatos, 177–179, figs. 52–54; Neils & Oakley, *Age*, no, 117.

GELA, 8678. *Para* 249; *Ta Attika*, 289.F33 (parts of BD).

RICHMOND, 60.11. *Para* 250. Shapiro, *Southern Collections*, 67, no. 24.

XIIIA. THE HAIMON PAINTER

Large cylinders

241.1 NEW YORK, 41.162.13 (once Gallatin). *ABV* 538; *BAdd* 133; *GRBS*, 31
(1990) pl. 9B at p. 160 (part).

Slender, with calyx-shaped mouth

241.5 LEIDEN, XV.II.20 (PC 32) (once Canino, 1345). *Acta Hungaricae*, 8
(1960) 12, fig. 4 (drawing); *CV* 2, pl. 105.1–6; *DialHist*, 10 (1984) 233, fig. 23,
235, fig. 26; *LIMC*, V, pl. 432, Iason 59 (part); *LIMC*, VII, 275, Pelias 16B;
Meyer, *Medeia,* pl. 16.2 (drawing); De Puma and Penny Small, *Murlo*, 191, fig.
17.3 (drawing).

241.6 CHIUSI, Bonci Casuccini. Meyer, *Medeia,* pl. 17.1 (drawing).

241.7, pl. 41.4 PARIS, CA 111. *LIMC*, VIII, pl. 805, Sphinx 174 (part of BD);
Moret, *Sphinx*, pl. 8.1–2.

241.8 SYRACUSE, 12085. Boardman, *ABFV*, fig. 273; Moret, *Sphinx*, pl. 8.2.

241.9, 130 ATHENS, 12954. Moret, *Sphinx*, pl. 8.3.

241.10 VIENNA, 190. Moret, *Sphinx*, pl. 9.2–4.

241.13 BONN, 358. *ABV* 538.

241.14, pl. 41.2A–B ATHENS, 472. *ABV* 539.

241.16 GENEVA, I 689.1891. *CV* 2, pl. 76.16–18.

242.18 HEIDELBERG, L 26. *CV* 4, pl. 174.4–6.

242.22 KARLSRUHE, 3050. *ABV* 538; *CV* 1, pl. 13.7–8.

242.23 FRANKFURT, LHaus, 532 (once Munich, Furtwängler). Bol, *Liebieghaus*, 46, figs. 47, 48; *CV* 2, pl. 49.8–10; *LIMC*, VII, pl. 522, Sarpedon 10 (parts); Shapiro, *Personifications*, 139, figs. 92–93.

242.26 NEW YORK, 41.162.78 (once Gallatin). *ABV* 538.

242.29 CAMBRIDGE, GR 105.1864 (G 130).

242.30, 117.3 NEW YORK, 41.162.246 (once Gallatin). *ABV* 514, 669; *BAdd* 148.

242.33 SAN SIMEON, 9493. *ABV* 538; *Para* 269.

242.35 CAMBRIDGE, GR 48.1937 (48.37). *ABV* 538; *BAdd* 133; *CV* 2, pl. 18.9; Darracott, *Ricketts and Shannon*, no. 57.

243.38 ATHENS, 464. *ABV* 538, 553.392; *BAdd* 133, 135; *Hephaistos*, 10 (1991) 69, no.20 (drawing of part).

243.39 ATHENS, 492. *ABV* 538.

243.43 NEW YORK, 41.162.217 (once Gallatin). *ABV* 538.

243.44 NEW YORK (once Gallatin). *ABV* 538.

243.50 ATHENS, 626. Schnapp, *Chasseur* 232, no.146 (drawing of BD).

243.52 PARIS, F 452. *LIMC*, VII, pl. 196, Peleus 145 (part).

243.54 KARLSRUHE, B 1530 (173). *ABV* 538; *LIMC*, V, pl. 632, Helios 8 (part); Manakidou, *Parastaseis*, pl. 37a (part).

243.57, 121.15 ATHENS, Market. *AK*, 5 (1962) pl. 17.1 (part); Dörig & Gigon, *Titanen*, pl. 24A; *Hephaistos*, 2 (1980) pl. 1C at p. 118.

Small lekythoi that recall the Diosphos Painter

244.66 BOLOGNA, 1195 (PU 211). *CV* 2, pl. 40.4.

24467 BRUSSELS, A 2193. *ABV* 706; *CV* 2, pl. 21.26 (part).

Miniatures

244.69 CAMBRIDGE, GR 73.1864 (95 not 96). *Para* 233; *BAdd* 124; *LIMC*, VII, pl. 195, Peleus 144 (part).

Of little-lion shape

244.71 DELOS, 567. *Para* 229.

'Chimney-mouthed' lekythoi

244.74 GÖTTINGEN, J 21. Mertens, *White Ground*, pl. 38.1 (part).

244.75 FRANKFURT, MusVF, β 305. Moret, *Sphinx*, pl. 27.1–2.

244.76 BERLIN, not known where, 4526. Moret, *Sphinx*, pl. 27.3.

245.77 TÜBINGEN, S.10/1292 (D 72). Berard, *Anodoi,* pl. 5, fig. 19; *CV* 3, pl. 50.4–6; *LIMC*, II, pl. 737, Athena 276; *LIMC*, III, pl. 300, Dionysos 53 (part).

245.80 PARIS, CA 2218. *Anz,* 1971, 170, figs. 10, 11, 12.

245.81 OXFORD, 1927.4457. Kurtz, *AWL*, pl. 70.4; *LIMC*, VII, pl. 703, Kyknos I 104 (parts); Mannack, *Einführung*, 125, fig. 74 (part).

245.82 AMPURIAS, 3829 (once Gerona). *ABV* 555.422; *BAdd* 135; *Arte Griego, 104*, 129, figs. 130, 165; Trias de Arribas pl. 43.1–2.

245.83, 134, pl. 41.3 ATHENS, 12768 (N 977). *ABV* 555.423.

245.84 BOLOGNA, 149. *CV* 2, pl. 44.1; Callipolitis-Feytmans, *Plats*, pl. 92.3. *Guida Bologna*, 283, top right; Schnapp, *Chasseur* 263, no.222 (I).

245.85 HAMBURG, 1906.164 (70). *ABV* 567.631; *BAdd* 136.

245.86 HAMBURG, 1906.165 (71). From Boeotia, Levadhia. *ABV* 567.630; *BAdd* 136; *LIMC*, IV, pl. 135, Gigantes 263A.

245.87 LONDON, B 350. *Para* 283.

245.88 LONDON, B 356. Boardman, *ABFV*, fig. 276; *Para* 283.

Mugs

(a) With two handles

245.89 OXFORD, 1879.157 (239). *ABV* 557.460.

245.91 PARIS, CabMed, 349. *ABV* 558.469.

245.92 PARIS, F 475. *ABV* 558.471.

245.93 OXFORD, 1884.707. *ABV* 558.472; *BAdd* 136.

246.94 OXFORD, 1879.158 (240A). *ABV* 557.449.

246.95 MUNICH, 1998 (J 1140). *ABV* 558.473.

246.96 LEIDEN, PC 71 (II.1693). *ABV* 558.479; *Para* 271; *BAdd* 136.

246.97 PARIS, F 478. *ABV* 557.466.

(β) Without handles

246.98 PARIS, CabMed, 351. *ABV* 559.501.

246.99 WARSAW (once Goluchow, Czartorski, 31). *ABV* 558.485.

246.100 UNKNOWN (once Rome, Candelori). *ABV* 559.486; *Anz*, 1937, 502, fig. 5 (drawing).

246.101 LEIDEN, K 96.9.5 (XVc 20). *ABV* 559.487; *BAdd* 136.

246.102 BASEL, BS 1921.348. *ABV* 559.494; *BAdd* 136.

246.103 NAPLES, 86389 (RC 175). *ABV* 559.504.

246.104 LEIDEN, K 94.9.37 (XVc 19). *ABV* 559.505; *BAdd* 136.

MUGS CLOSELY RELATED TO THE HAIMON PAINTER

(a) With two handles

246.1 BOLOGNA, 124. *ABV* 557.464.

246.3 PARIS, F 428. *ABV* 558.475.

(b) Without handles

246.4 PARIS, F 429. *ABV* 559.507.

246.5 NEW YORK, GR 555. *ABV* 559.489.

246.6 WARSAW (once Goluchow, Czartorski, 215). *ABV* 559.503.

246.7 NEW YORK, 06.1021.65 (once Paris, market, Platt). *ABV* 558.480.

246.8 PARIS, F 426. *ABV* 559.508.

A LEKYTHOS NEAR THE HAIMON PAINTER, SHOWING A CERTAIN RELATIONSHIP TO THE DIOSPHOS PAINTER

247 NEW YORK, 41.162.255 (once Gallatin). *CV* Hoppin & Gallatin, pl. 8 (28).1, 3; *Classical Antiquity*, 12 (1993) fig. 11 at p. 266 (part).

ADDENDA TO BEAZLEY'S ATTRIBUTIONS TO THE HAIMON PAINTER

538.1 PRINCETON, 51.43. *AJA* 103 (1999) 250, fig. 30 (part).

538.2 NEW YORK, 34.11.6. *Para* 269; *BAdd* 133; Shapiro, *Personifications*, 153, fig. 112 (part).

Manner of the Haimon Painter

539.2 OLYMPIA, 2902. *Olympische Forschungen*, 28 (2000) pl. 84.250 (BD).

540.28 TARANTO, 52349. *Para* 274; *Taranto* I.3, 305, no.83.2.

540.42 WASHINGTON, 391053. Schwarz, *Washington*, pl. 28, no.18.

540.45 SIENA, 38444 (once Siena, Chigi). *Para* 269; Cygielman and Mangani, pl. 14, no.20.

540.53 NEW YORK, Sotheby's (once Boston, 76.449). *SothPB*, 12.6.2001, 156–157, no.259.

541.59 BERNE, 23294. Jucker, *Antikensammlung*, pl. 16.46

541.66 COPENHAGEN, 7763. *LIMC*, V, pl. 233, Hermes 426a (part).

541.68 GENEVA, I 744. *BAdd* 134; *CV*, I, pl. 75.13–15; Birchler Emery, *Musique*, pls. 14–15.67 (parts).

542.115 LONDON, B 647. *Ta Attika*, 293.F50 (parts).

543.131 HAVANA, 142 (once Lagunillas). Olmos, *Habana*, 146, no.63.

543.145 WASHINGTON, 391051. Schwarz, *Washington*, pl. 25. no. 14.

544.152 BERNE, 23296. Jucker, *Antikensammlung*, pl. 17.47.

544.158 ATHENS, Agora, P 10575. *Hesperia*, 62 (1993) pl. 81B (part).

544.161 LEIDEN RO.II.2 (XV.J.123). *BAdd* 134; Bastet, *Rottiers*, pl. 15.168 (part).

544.162 WASHINGTON, 391052. Schwarz, *Washington*, pl. 24, no. 13.

544.165 BARCELONA, 373. *BAdd* 134; *Arte Griego*, 13, fig. 3, 113, fig. 144 (part); Trias de Arribas, pl. 27.3.

545.182 OLYMPIA, 2901. *Olympische Forschungen*, 28 (2000) pl. 82.218 (BD).

545.196 NEW YORK, Sotheby's (once Boston, 76.448). *SothPB*, 12.6.2001, 169, no.259.2 (part).

546.213 THEBES, 17085 (R.46.63 **not** R.46.43). *LIMC*, IV, pl. 122, Gigantes 149 (parts); *CV*, pls. 67.1–3, 69.19.

546.218 THEBES, 17088 (R46.62). *LIMC*, IV, pl. 134, Gigantes 261N (part); *CV*, pls. 67.4–6, 69.20.

546.219 BERNE, 23247. Jucker, *Antikensammlung,* pl. 17.48; *LIMC*, IV, pl. 135, Gigantes 262H (part).

546.222 BALTIMORE, 48.228. *LIMC*, IV, pl. 134, Gigantes 262D (part).

547.231 BERNE, 23298. Jucker, *Antikensammlung*, pl. 17.45.

548.263 MADRID, 36303. *Arte Griego*, 118, fig. 153; Trias de Arribas, pl. 147.2.

548.278 CHAMPAIGN-URBANA, 22.1.122. *CV*, pl. 12.

550.307 OLYMPIA, 2892. *Olympische Forschungen*, 28 (2000) pl. 83.232 (BD) [same vase ?].

550.310 GLASGOW 1902.73AR. *CV*, pl. 24.8–10 (BD).

550.317 NEW HAVEN, 1913.116. *BAdd* 135; *LIMC*, V, pl. 442, Io I2; *RA*, 1990, 1, 11, figs. 6–8.

550.318 BALTIMORE, 48.230. *LIMC*, V, pl. 492, Iris I 86 (part).

552.352 BARCELONA, 4713. *BAdd* 135; *RA*, 88 (1986) 376, fig. 55B (part).

551.333 CAMBRIDGE (MA) 1960.330. (once Oxford (MS), Robinson), *BAdd* 135; *LIMC*, VI, pl. 629, Odysseus I12 (part).

552.359 GENEVA, 10847. *BAdd* 135; Birchler Emery, *Musique*, pls. 14, 16.68 (parts).

552.363 GLASGOW, 1902.73AQ. *CV*, pl. 24.11–13 (BD).

553.391 PARIS, CA 1928. *BAdd* 135; *LIMC*, V, pl. 304, Hippalektryon 47.

553.393 ATHENS, Agora, P 17063. Berard, *Images et société*, 91, fig. 3, 97, pls. 1A, 2A, 3B (BD, drawings).

553.396 GENEVA, 15001. *BAdd* 135; Birchler Emery, *Musique*, pl. 15.66 (BD).

554.410 OLYMPIA, 2900. *Olympische Forschungen*, 28 (2000) pl. 83.226 (BD).

554.416 AMPURIAS (once Barcelona). *BAdd* 135; *Arte Griego*, 84, fig. 98, 124, fig. 159; Trias de Arribas, pl. 31.3.

556.437 RHODES, 10784. *Para* 270, 283, 289; *Potters and Painters*, 461, fig. 5 left (BD).

556.438 RHODES, 10785. *Para* 270, 283, 289; *Potters and Painters*, 461, fig. 5 right.

556.442BIS BERLIN, F 2034.*BAdd* 136; *CV*, 7, pls. 44.7, 45.4–6, Beilage K; *LIMC*, V, pl. 60, Herakles 2094 (part); Brommer, *Heracles*, pl. 17 (part).

556.442TER BERLIN, F 2035. *BAdd* 136; *CV*, 7, pls. 44.6, 45.1–3, Beilage K.

556 BRUSSELS, A 1907. *Para* 284; Balty, *Animaux*, 205, no.259.

557.2 MONTPELLIER, SA 136 (191A). *BAdd* 136; Laurens, *Montpellier*, pls. 28–29; *Vases a Mémoire*, 146, no.96.

557.454 FLORENCE, 3868. *Firenze, Vasi Attici*, 56, fig. 81 (colour of A).

557.465 MUNICH, 2000 (J 59). *Para* 271; *Kunst der Schale*, 407, fig. 72.4.

558.467 TOULOUSE, 26.104 (S 353). *Musée Saint-Raymond*, 55, no.36 (A).

558.470 BERKELEY, 8.891. *CV*, 1, pl. 18.3.

559.492 CAMBRIDGE (MA), 1927.141. Berard, *Images et société*, 126, fig. 8 (part, drawing of part); *LIMC*, V, pl. 61, 77, Herakles 2100 (B), Herakles 2342 (A).

560.516 HEIDELBERG, 599. *BAdd* 136; *Jb*, 105 (1990) 107, fig. 9 (A).

560.518 UPPSALA, 1628 (once Stockholm, National Museum). *BAdd* 136; *AK*, 19 (1976) pl. 5.1.3.5 (I, A, B); Berard, *Images et société*, 96,fig. 10 (A, part of B).

561.541 ATHENS, 357 (CC 1108). *BAdd* 136; *LIMC*, VII, pl. 366, Poseidon 163 (A).

562.557 READING, 26.VII.2. *LIMC*, V, pl. 79, Herakles 2349 (A).

564.580 ATHENS, 505 (CC 1093). *LIMC*, VII, pl. 616, Thanatos 13 (A); Shapiro, *Personifications*, 138, fig. 91 (A).

565.595 LECCE, 568. Semeraro, *Salento arcaico*, 89, fig. 46 (A)

566.612 OXFORD, 1951.359. Lissarrague, *Céramique*, 478, fig. 4 (A); *LIMC*, IV, pl. 137, Gigantes 285 (A).

566.616 LECCE, 561. *Para* 271; Delli Ponti, *Lecce*, 20, fig. 13 (A).

566.624 PLOVDIV, 1212. *Para* 271; Lazarow, *Bulgaria*, 48, no.11 (A).

567.628 SALERNO, 332 B. Greco and Pontrandolfo, *Fratte*, 246, fig. 411 (A).

568.644 ATHENS, 17529. *Para* 271; *CV*, 4, pl. 64.3–4.

(569.594BIS), 707 ATHENS, Agora, P 22986. *BAdd* 236; *LIMC*, VI, pl. 558, Nike 10 (I).

569.660 ATHENS, 18640 (E 1851). *BAdd* 137; *CV*, 4, pl. 64.1–2, fig. 16.4.

569.661 ATHENS, Agora, P 23321. *BAdd* 137; *Hesperia*, 62 (1993) pl. 81D (A).

569.669 BARCELONA, 431. *BAdd* 137; *Arte Griego*, 118, fig. 154; Trias de Arribas, pl. 47.4.

569.670 ADRIA, 22511 (A 184) (S 55). *CV*, 2, pl. 33.2.

571.703 GENEVA, 14996. *BAdd* 137; Birchler Emery, *Musique*, pl. 16.69 (A).

571.709, 628.11 ATHENS, 18809 (E 1193). *Para* 309; *BAdd* 137; *CV*, 4, fig. 16.2, pl. 63.1–3.

572.4 CAMBRIDGE (MA), 1960.329 (once Oxford (MS), Robinson). *Para* 287; *BAdd* 137; *LIMC*, V, pl. 568, Kaineus 29 (part).

572.7 PARIS, CabMed, 306. *Para* 294; *BAdd* 138; Grabow, *Schlangenbilder*, pl. 18.K84 (drawing); *Ktema*, 15 (1990) pl. 4.1–2 at p. 154 (parts); *LIMC*, VII, pl. 489, Python 3 (part).

(571) SIENA, 38443 (once Chigi). *Para* 272; Cygielman and Mangani, pl. 14, no.19 (BD).

(571) TARANTO, 4427. *Para* 275; *Taranto I.3*, 313, no.96.1 (BD).

(571) CORINTH, T 1672. *Para* 277; *Hesperia*, 64 (1995) pl. 91.6 (part).

(571) STUTTGART, 4.96 (KAS 89). *Para* 277; *LIMC*, pl. 61, Herakles 2095.

(571) ATHENS, 12395 (N 931). *Para* 280; *BAdd* 135; *Hephaistos*, 10 (1991) 69, no.21 (drawing of part); Berard, *Images et société*, 92, figs. 6–7, 97–100, pls. 1B, 2C, 3C, 4C (part, drawings).

(571) WÜRZBURG, HA 917 (L 378). *Para* 281; Berard, *Images et société*, 89, fig. 1.

(571) BERLIN, 3356. *Para* 281; Berard, *Images et société*, 97, 100, pls. 1D, 4A (drawings of BD).

(571) SOUTH HADLEY, 9.1909 (once Poughkeepsie (N.Y.), Vassar College, BAIV 9). *Para* 281; Berard, *Images et société*, 92, figs. 6–7, 98, pl. 2B (drawings, part).

(571) BARCELONA, 376. *Para* 282; *BAdd* 135; *Arte Griego*, 57, fig. 61; Trias de Arribas, pl. 31.4.

(571) FRANKFURT, β 311. *Para* 285; *CV*, 2, pls. 56.4, 57.1–2.

(571) NEW YORK, 57.12.5. *Para* 285; *LIMC*, VIII, pl. 743, Seirenes 117 (A).

(571) ATHENS, Agora, P 24472. *Para* 228, 281; *BAdd* 123; Carpenter, *Fifth-Century Imagery*, pl. 39A (part).

(571) GELA, 12353. *Para* 271; *Ta Attika*, 294.F51 (parts of BD).

(571) GELA, 8675. *Para* 272; *Ta Attika*, 294.F52 (parts of BD).

(571) GELA, 16. *Para* 278; *Ta Attika*, 295.F54.

(571) SYRACUSE. *Para* 280; *BAdd* 135; *Ta Attika*, 295.F55 (drawing of BD).

(571) GELA, 12354. *Para* 282; *Ta Attika*, 295.F56.

Connected to the Haimon Group

572.1 LONDON, 1895.10–29.1. *BAdd* 137; *LIMC*, V, pl. 85, Herakles 2472.

573.4 MOSCOW, 19308 (H 414). *Para* 287; *Potters and Painters*, 128, fig. 5 (BD).

573.8, 441.5 NAPLES, 81169 (H 2731) (M 980). *Potters and Painters*, 134, fig. 22 (BD).

573.10 PARIS, CP 10864. *Para* 287; *Potters and Painters*, 132, fig. 18; Fournier-Christol, *Olpes*, pl. 45, no.73.

Near the Haimon Group

574.1 BALTIMORE, 48.234. *LIMC*, IV, pl. 135, Gigantes 262E (parts).

574.2 ATHENS, Ceramicus, 702.*LIMC*, IV, pl. 134, Gigantes 262A (parts).

574.2 HEIDELBERG, L 29. *Para* 289; *BAdd* 138; *LIMC*, VII, pl. 703, Kyknos I 103.

Compare the Haimon Painter

429.9 MUNICH, 1810 (J 122). *CV,* 12, pl. 50.1–3, BEILAGE 17.2.

XIIIB. LEKYTHOI OF THE PHOLOS GROUP

The first type

247.1 BERKELEY, 8.35 (once Somzee). *CV* 1, pl. 27.3; Stern, *Labours*, no. 7; Uhlenbrock, *Herakles*, pl. 19.

The third type

247.5 PARIS, CabMéd, 308 (once Oppermann, 41). *CV* 2, pl. 86.1,3–5; *Hommes, Dieux et Héros*, 234–35, figs. 96A–B.

247.8 COPENHAGEN, B 78 (VIII 948). *CV* 3, pl. 111.18.

247.10 PARIS, MNB 2039 (L 29). Pelling, *Tragedy*, pl. 5 (part).

A LINK BETWEEN THE HAIMON PAINTER AND THE PHOLOS GROUP

248 ODESSA, 26650. *ABV* 708; *BAdd* 137.

ADDENDA TO BEAZLEY'S ATTRIBUTIONS TO THE PHOLOS PAINTER

572.4 CAMBRIDGE (MA), 1960.329 (once Oxford (MS), Robinson). *Para* 287; *BAdd* 137; *LIMC*, V, pl. 568, Kaineus 29 (part).

Near the Pholos Painter

572.7 PARIS, CabMed, 306. *Para* 294; *BAdd* 137; Grabow, *Schlangenbilder*, pl. 18.K84 (drawing); *LIMC*, VII, pl. 489, Python 3 (part); *Ktema*, 15 (1990) pl. 1–2 at p. 54 (parts).

XIIIbis. THE PAINTER OF THE HALF-PALMETTES

248.1 LONDON, B 349. *Potters and Painters*, 129, fig. 9 (BD); *CV* 6, pl. 97 (356).3; *LIMC*, VII, pl. 190, Peleus 87; *Acta Upsaliensis* 2 (1978) 64, fig. 10.

248.2 LONDON, B 354. *Potters and Painters*, 128, fig. 6 (drawing of BD); *CV* 6, pl. 97 (356).6.

248.5 LONDON, B 359. *Anz*, 1974, 155, fig. 6; *Potters and Painters*, 135, fig. 25 (BD); *CV* 6, pl. 97 (356).11; Kurtz, *AWL*, pl. 62.1; *LIMC*, II, pl. 737, Athena 277.

248.6 LONDON, 1864.10–7.184. *Potters and Painters*, 127, fig. 3 (drawing of BD); *CV* 6, pl. 98 (357).7.

248.9 LONDON, 1864.10–7.1715. *Potters and Painters*, 126, fig. 1 (BD); *CV* 6, pl. 98 (357).12.

248.11 BERLIN, F 1930. *ABV* 573.2; *Para* 287; *BAdd* 137; *Potters and Painters*, 131, fig. 14 (drawing of BD); Hamdorf, *Dionysos*, 33, fig. 8 (drawing).

248.12 PARIS, CabMed, 267. *ABV* 573.3; *Para* 287; *Potters and Painters*, 130, fig. 11 (part).

248.13 SEVRES, 91. *ABV* 573.4; *CV*, pl. 16.11; *Proceedings*, fig. 21 (drawing of part).

248.14 LONDON, B 505. *ABV* 573.6.

248.15 TÜBINGEN S.10/1295 (D 62). *ABV* 573.1; *BAdd* 137; *Potters and Painters*, 135, fig. 23 (BD); Cesare, *Statue in Immagine*, 168, fig. 104 (BD).

ADDENDA TO BEAZLEY'S ATTRIBUTIONS TO THE PAINTER OF THE HALF-PALMETTES

573.4 MOSCOW, HistMus, 19308. *Para* 287; *Potters and Painters*, 128, fig. 5 (BD).

708.4BIS NAPLES, M 885. *Potters and Painters*, 132, fig. 16 (drawing of BD).

441.5, 573.8 NAPLES, M 980. *Potters and Painters*, 134, fig. 22 (BD).

573.10 PARIS, CP 10864. *Para* 287; *Potters and Painters*, 132, fig. 18; Fournier-Christol, *Olpes*, pl. 45, no. 73.

COPENHAGEN, 6446. *Para* 287; *Potters and Painters*, 129, fig. 7 (BD).

FRANKFURT, MusVF, β 308. *Para* 287, 288; *Potters and Painters*, 132, fig. 17 (drawing of BD).

BERLIN, F 1929. *BAdd* 137; *Para* 288; *Potters and Painters*, 127 (BD).

BERNE, Jucker. *Para* 288; *Potters and Painters*, 133, fig. 19 (drawing of BD).

ROME, Capitolini, 66. *Para* 288; *BAdd* 138; *Potters and Painters*, 134, fig. 21 (BD).

FERRARA, 158. *Para* 288; *BAdd* 137; *Potters and Painters*, 133, fig. 20 (drawing of BD).

429.9 MUNICH, 1810. *CV* 12, pl. 50.1–3, BEILAGE 17.2.

XIV. THE THESEUS PAINTER

249.1, 142, 163, 179 ATHENS, Acr., 1280. Kerenyi, K., *Dionysos* (London, 1976) fig. 29 (drawing of A).

249.2 LAON, 37.996 (Once Paris, market). *ABV* 703; *Para* 255.

249.3 DELOS, B 6.138 (595). Wolf, *Herakles,* figs. 61–63 (A, B); Hadjidakis, *Delos,* 364, no.700.

249.4 ATHENS, Agora, P 1545. *ABV* 518.4; *BAdd* 129; Wolf, *Herakles,* fig. 68 (A).

249.6 NAPLES, 81154 (H 2468). *ABV* 703; *LIMC,* V, pl. 146, Herakles 3239 (A); *Modi e Funzioni,* 196, fig. 13 (A); Wolf, *Herakles,* figs. 93–96 (A, B).

249.8 DELOS, 598. *Para* 255; Hadjidakis, *Delos,* 363, no. 699.

249.9 LONDON, 1902.12–18.3. Boardman, *ABFV,* fig. 246; *LIMC,* II, pl. 725, Athena 181 (part); *LIMC,* V, pl. 141, Herakles 3161 (A); Boardman, *History,* 65, fig. 85 (A).

249.10 DRESDEN, ZV 1680. *AK,* 43 (2000) pl. 7.1 (A).

250.11 BASEL, Kämbli (once Pfuhl). *Para* 255.

250.12 ATHENS, Acr., 1265. *Acta Upsaliensi,* 2 (1978) 68, fig. 1 (part).

250.13 ATHENS, Acr., 1312. *Acta Upsaliensis,* 2 (1978) 68, fig. 1 (part).

250.16 THE HAGUE, 2135. *Potters and Painters,* 131, fig. 15 (drawing of BD)

250.17 TARANTO, 4448 (7030). *ABV* 518; *Para* 255; *BAdd* 129; *CV* 2, pl. 11; *LIMC,* V, pl. 221, Hermes 246 (B); Lippolis, *Eroi,* 20, fig. 9 (colour of A); Schefold and Jung, *Urkönige,* 193, fig. 236 (A); *Taranto* I.2, pl. 2 (colour of B); *Taranto* I.3, 52, 56, 228–229, no. 42.18 (including colour of parts A and B).

250.20 LIMENAS, Museum. *Para* 255.

250.21, 120.2 TARANTO, 4457 (7029). *ABV* 518; *BAdd* 129; *LIMC,* V, pls. 91–92, Herakles 2546 (A, B); Schefold and Jung, *Urkönige,* 162, fig. 197 (A); *Taranto* 3.1, 29, fig. 15 (drawing); *Taranto* I.3, 55, 227, no. 42.17 (including colour of A).

250.22 NEW YORK, 17.230.9. *ABV* 703.

250.24 BONN, 1646. *ABV* 518, *AK* 43 (2000) pl. 5.3 (A).

250.25, 143, 144 ATHENS, Acr., 1306. *BABesch,* 58 (1983) 60, fig. 5; *Fest Brommer,* pl. 81.1 (drawing); Schefold and Jung, *Urkönige,* 199, fig. 245.

250.26 BOSTON, 99.523. *ABV* 518.

250.27 LONDON, 1920.2–16.3. *Para* 93.3.

250.28 ST. PETERSBURG, 1912. Gorbunova, *Chernofigurnie,* 149, no. 119 (A).

250.29 ATHENS, Acr., 1281. *Solon to Salamis*, 93, fig. 4 (drawing); Boardman, *ABFV*, fig. 247 (drawing); Hedreen, *Silens*, pl. 2 (drawing of A); Kenner, *Verkehrte Welt*, 80, fig. 28 (drawing); Kerenyi, *Dionysos*, fig. 57 (drawing); *LIMC*, III, pl. 492, Dionysos 827 (drawing); Pickard-Cambridge, fig. 7a; Pickard-Cambridge2, fig. 12; Pickard-Cambridge, *Dithyramb*, fig. 7; *QuadTic*, 12 (1983) 109, pl. 1 (drawing); *QuadTic*, 9 (1980) 56, pl. 5 (drawing). Schöne, *Thiasos*, pl. 30.2 (drawing); Steinhart, *Auge*, pl. 36.2 (drawing).

250.30 LONDON, B 79. *Solon to Salamis*, 93, fig. 5 (drawing); Bieber, *Theater,* 19, fig. 56 (drawing of A, B, restored); Crouwel, *Chariots*, pl. 26.2 (drawing of part); Guazzelli, *Antesterie,* fig. 16 (drawing); *JHS*, 78 (1958) 6, fig. 3 (drawing of A); Kerenyi, *Dionysos*, figs. 58, 59A, B (part and drawing of A, B); *LIMC*, III, pl. 398, Dionysos 828 (A); Pickard-Cambridge, fig. 7B at p. 16 (drawing of A, restored); Pickard-Cambridge2, fig. 13 (drawing of B); Pickard-Cambridge, *Dithyramb*, figs. 5–6, at p. 114 (A, B); *QuadTic*, 12 (1983) 113, pl. 3 (drawing of A); van Straten, *Hiera Kala,* fig. 10 (drawing).

250.31 UNIVERSITY, 1977.3.697 (once Robinson). *Para* 255; *Ephemeris*, 127 (1988) 134, fig. 15b (A).

250.33 NAPLES, 81159. *Para* 255; *BAdd*, 129; Brinkmann, *Beobachtungen*, 83 (drawings of A and B); *CV* 1, pl. 46, figs. 1–2 (A, B); Grabow, *Schlangenbilder*, pl. 9.K49 (drawing).

250.34 LECCE, 560. *Para* 255.

250.35 BOLOGNA, 129. *ABV* 703; *Para* 255; *Ephemeris*, 127 (1988) 134, fig. 15a (drawing).

251.36 WINCHESTER, 12. *ABV* 518; *CV*, pl. 3.5–8; Mannack, *Einführung*, 125, fig.75 (A).

251.39 ELEUSIS, 314. *Para* 255.

251.40 GREIFSWALD, 197. *ABV* 518.

251.43 NEW YORK, 06.1021.49. *ABV* 703; *BAdd* 61, 129; Immerwahr, *Attic Script*, pl. 24.103 (part of A); *LIMC*, VI, pl. 519, Nereus 15 (A); Vanhove, *deporte*, 346, no. 213 (colour pl. of A and B); Poliakoff, *Combat Sports*, 58, fig. 56 (A, part of B); Vanhove, *Sport* 346, no. 213 (colour of A and B).

251.44, 142 ATHENS, 498 (CC 1001). *CV* 1, pl. 4 (12).1–3; *La Cité des Images*, 136, fig. 190 (A, B, side); Kachler, *Theatermaske*, 43, figs. 15–17 (A, B, side); Kerenyi, *Dionysos*, fig. 76A,B, C (A, B, side).

251.47 ATHENS, Agora, P 1544. *ABV* 518; *BAdd* 129.

251.48 ATHENS, Agora, P 1548. *ABV* 518; *BAdd* 129.

251.48BIS ATHENS, Agora, P 1549. *ABV* 518; *BAdd* 129.

251.49 ATHENS, Agora, P 1547. *ABV* 518; *BAdd* 129.

251.50 COPENHAGEN, 6571. Beck, *Album*, pl. 65.332 (side); *CV* 3, pl. 119.9.

251.51 BRUSSELS, R 327. *ABV* 518; May, *Jouer,* 118, fig. 110 (colour of A).

251.52 AMSTERDAM, 2178. *CV* Scheurleer 2, pl. 6 (75).5–9; Vanhove, *deporte* 172, no. 25; Vanhove, *Sport* 172, no. 25.

251.54 ATHENS, Agora, P 1546. *ABV* 518; *BAdd* 129; *Mind and Body*, 198, no. 89 (A); Valavanis and Kourkoumelis, *Chaire*, 99 (colour of A).

251.55 CAMBRIDGE. *Para* 255.

251.56 NAPLES. *ABV* 703.

251.57 BRUSSELS, A 1953. *ABV* 518; *Para* 255; *BAdd* 129; Shapiro, *Personifications*, 152, fig. 11 (part).

252.58, 142–143, 145, 149, pl. 43.1A–B ATHENS, 515. *ABV* 518; *AM*, 103 (1988) 103, fig. 32 (part).

252.59, pl. 42.4 SYRACUSE, 33501. *Ta Attika,* 290.F37 (part).

252.65, 120.8 OXFORD, 1934.372. *LIMC*, VIII, pl. 672, Polyphemos I 45; Touchefeu-Meynier, *Themes Odysseens*, pl. 10.2–4; Wijer, *Polyphemusavontuur*, no. 136.

252.66, pl. 44.3 BONN, 307. *ABV* 518; *Para* 255.66; *BCH*, 92 (1968) 570, fig. 20; Delavaud-Roux, *Danses Armées,* 99, no. 25 (part); *Jb*, 105 (1990) 179, fig. 9 (part).

252.67, pl. 44.1 BERLIN, F 2005. *LIMC*, VII, pl. 109, Paridis iudicium 17 (part).

252.68 LONDON, 1904.7–8.5. Ahlberg-Cornell, *Myth,* 299, fig. 67 (part).

252.70, pl. 42.3 PARIS, F 342. *ABV* 433.6, 697, 704; *BAdd* 111; Garland, *Deformity,* fig. 39 (part); *Jb*, 103 (1988) 189, figs. 15–16 (A, B); *LIMC*, VI, pl. 72, Kyklops, Kyklopes 18; Andreae, *Ulisse*, 48, fig. 8A–B (colour); Buitron, *Odyssey*, 44–45, no. 10.

252.71 ATHENS, 13262. *ABV* 450.1.

252.72 LONDON, B 346. *CV* 6, 12, fig. A (drawing); *LIMC*, VI, pl. 388, Mousa, Mousai 36B; *Acta Upsaliensis* 2 (1978) fig. 8.

252.73 MADRID, 10930 (once Salamanca). *CV* 1, pl. 29.3; *LIMC*, II, pl. 241, Apollon 700.

252.74 OXFORD, 1930.620. *CV* 3, pl. 25.5.

252.76, 146 WINCHESTER, 8. *ABV* 520.35, *CV*, pl. 2.4–6 (A, B, I).

252.77 COPENHAGEN, 106 (VIII 457). From Vulci. *ABV* 207; *Para* 98; *BAdd* 56.

253.1 PHILADELPHIA, 5481. *AJA*, 26 (1922) 174–5, figs. 1–2 (A, B); *Aspects of Ancient Greece*, 52, 53, no. 23 (A); *JHS*, 75 (1955) pl. 9, figs. 1–2 (A, B);

LIMC, VI, pl. 489, Nereides 261; *Museum Journal, Philadelphia*, (1919) 16–17, figs. 6–7 (A, B); Uhlenbrock, *Herakles*, pl. 18 (A).

253.3 LONDON, 1926.11–15.1. Bothmer, *Amazons*, pl. 40.1–2 (A,B); *Bestattungswesen*, 319, fig. 4 (B); *LIMC*, I, pl. 447, Amazones 57 (A).

253.4 PARIS, MusRodin, 1000.244 (492). *ABV* 521.1; *BAdd* 130.

253.5 CAMBRIDGE (MA), 60.324 (once Sheffield, Mr. A.M. Woodward). *AJA*, 60 (1956) pl. 13, figs. 61–62.

253.6 PARIS, CA 792. *JHS*, 75 (1955) pl. 8, fig. 2 (B).

253.7 PARIS, CA 1812. *JHS*, 75 (1955) pl. 7, figs. 1, 4 (parts of A and B); *LIMC*, VI, pl. 237, Memnon 64 (A, B).

253.9 ROME, 3551. From Falerii. *ABV* 521.4.

253.10, 109 THEBES 17097 (R.18.99). *ABV* 522.1 (near the Painter of Rodin 1000); *CV*, 55, fig. 20, pl. 47.

253.11 ATHENS, 362 (CC 795). *ABV* 522.2; *CV* 4, fig. 10.3, pl. 35 (including profile).

253.15 BOLOGNA, 130 (DL 109). Bieber, *Theaterwesen*, 88, fig. 91 (drawing); Bieber, *Theater,* 19, fig. 58 (drawing); *CAH, Plates to Volumes 5&6*, 140, fig. 143 (drawing); *CV* 2, pl. 43.1–4; Guazzelli, *Antesterie*, fig. 17 (drawing); Kerenyi, *Dionysos,* fig. 56; *LIMC*, III, pl. 398, Dionysos 829 (drawing); Berti and Gasparri, 101.42 (A, B); Nilsson, *Religion*, pl. 36.1 (drawing); Pickard-Cambridge, 12, fig. 6 (drawing); Pickard-Cambridge2, 13, fig. 11 (drawing); Pickard-Cambridge, *Dithyramb*, 83, 113, figs. 3–4 (drawing); Parke, *Festivals*, fig. 42 (part); *QuadTic*, 12 (1983) 111, pl. 2 (drawing); Schöne, *Thiasos*, pl. 30.1 (drawing); Simon, *Festivals*, 94, fig. 12 (drawing of part of A).

253.16 BERLIN, 3283. *ABV* 704; *Ausgestellte Werke*, 76, no. 11 (A); Andreae, *Ulisse*, 124, no. 2.6 (A, B); *LIMC*, VI, pl. 73, Kyklops, Kyklopes 22 (A); Buitron, *Odyssey*, 35, fig.19.

TWO LEKYTHOI BY ONE HAND

254.2, 146 LONDON, 78–1.20 (B 542). *LIMC*, VII, pl. 346, Polyxene 7 (parts).

254.3 SYRACUSE, 20901. *Ta Attika*, 291.F38 (parts).

LEKYTHOI IN HIS MANNER

254.1 OXFORD, G 246 (V 513). *Ta Attika*, 291.F38bis (part).

254.2 AGRIGENTO. *ABV* 521; *Para* 259.2.

ADDENDA TO BEAZLEY'S ATTRIBUTIONS TO THE THESEUS PAINTER

518.1 ARMONK, Pinney. *LIMC*, VIII, pl. 24, Tityos 5; *Para* 256.

518.2 ATHENS, Ceramicus, 1486 (5671). *BAdd* 129; *GRBS*, 32 (1991) pl. 1 at p.32 (parts); Hephaistos, 15 (1997) 63, fig.20 (parts); *AM*, 114 (1999) pl 10.2 (parts).

518.4 BOSTON, 1921.277. *LIMC*, V, pl. 138, Herakles 3122 (part), pl. 245, Hermes 548B (A).

518.5 HAVANA, 140. *BAdd* 129. Olmos, *Lagunillas*, 76, 78–79, no. 20.

519.7 BERLIN, 3230. *BAdd* 129; *Ausgestellte Werke*, 94, no. 12; *CV* 7, pl. 39.3–5, BEILAGE G (including profile).

519.8 DRESDEN, ZV 2006.

704.11BIS MUNICH, 1678. *Kunst der Schale*, 299, fig. 49.1A–B (A, B).

519.15 UPPSALA, 352. *BAdd* 129; Cesare, *Statue in Immagine*, 168, fig. 105 (BD); Garland, *Gods*, pl. 2. *LIMC*, II, pl. 767, Athena 581; Neils, *Parthenon Frieze*, 115, fig.117 (BD).

520.23 ATHENS, 18720. *BAdd* 129. *CV* 4, pls. 41, 43.1–2, fig. 12.1 (including profile).

520.24 BASEL, Cahn, HC 1469. *Para* 256; Kreuzer, *Frühe Zeichner*, 116, no. 124.

520.26 CAMBRIDGE (MA), 1960.321. *BAdd* 129; Angiolillo, *Pisistrato*, 105, fig. 50 (AH); *Fest Lauffer*, 3, 791, fig. 1, pl. 10 at p. 804; Fellmuth, *Jenaer Maler*, 19, fig. 14 (drawing); *Para* 256; Scheibler, *Töpferkunst*, 111, fig. 102 (drawing of A and B); Scheibler, *Töpferkunst2*, 111, fig. 102 (drawing of A and B).

520.32 LONDON, 1864.10–7.1686. *BAdd* 130. Christiansen and Melander, *Proceedings*, 345, fig. 10 (I); *LIMC*, IV, pl. 544, Herakles 1497 (B); Wolf, *Herakles*, figs. 39, 59 (A, B).

520.33 TARANTO, 6515. Cesare, *Statue in Immagine*, 57, fig. 11 (I); *LIMC*, IV, pl. 445, Herakles 15 (I); Shapiro, *Tyrants*, pl. 70B (I).

520.34 SALERNO, 158 A. Greco and Pontrandolfo, *Fratte*, 196, fig. 313 (I).

521 OLYMPIA, BE 634. *LIMC*, V, pl. 75, Herakles 2324 (A); *Olympische Forschungen*, 28 (2000) pl. 73.108 (A, B, UH, profile); Boardman, *History*, 288, fig. 314 (A); *Jb*, 103 (1988) 188, figs. 13–14 (A, B).

SAN ANTONIO, 86.134.157. *BAdd* 129; *Studi Nenci*, frontispiece (A); *Goddess and Polis*, 56, 95, no. 48 (A, B); *Para* 257; Shapiro, *San Antonio*, 114, no. 56 (A, B); *Sotheby-Parke-Bernet*, 8–9.2.1985, no. 66; *Sotheby*, 1.12.1969, no. 83 (A, B).

STUTTGART, KAS 74. *CV* 1, pls. 19.1–2, 20.1; *Para* 258.

BASEL, Cahn, HC 587. Kreuzer, *Frühe Zeichner*, no. 125; *Para* 258W.

ATHENS, British School, A 380. Oakley, *Gennadius*, 30, fig. 19; *Para* 259.

PARIS, CA1924. *BAdd* 130; Ghiron-Bistagne, *Recherches*, 261, figs. 111, 112 (A, B, I); *Para* 259.

TOLEDO, 63.27. *Para* 257; *BAdd* 129; Grabow, *Schlangenbilder*, pl. 15.K71 (A).

704.27TER TAMPA, 86.52. *Para* 256; *BAdd* 129; *Classical Antiquity*, 12 (1993) fig. 7 at p. 266 (A, B).

XV. VASES BY THE ATHENA PAINTER

160 BOSTON, 13.74 (R 355). *ABV* 530.84; *Para* 264.

254.1 ATHENS, 514 (CC 880). Shapiro, *Tyrants*, pl. 51C–D.

254.2 GENEVA, Hirsch. *ABV* 522.

254.3 LEIDEN, XV.82. *ABV* 522; *BAdd* 130; *LIMC*, V, pl. 239, Hermes 464C (part).

254.4 TARANTO, 4414. *Para* 236; *Taranto* I.3, 308, no. 87.1.

254.5 ST. LOUIS, 3279. *ABV* 522; *AJA* 44 (1940) 200, figs. 11–13.

255.7 LUZERN, Private (once Geneva market, Hirsch). *Para* 260.

255.8 KARLSRUHE, B 28 (172). *ABV* 522.

255.10 TARANTO, 4430. *Taranto* I.3, 308, no. 88.1 (part).

255.13 OXFORD, 1965.98 (once Northwick, Spencer-Churchill). *Para* 260; *LIMC*, IV, pl. 133, Gigantes 258C (part).

255.14 BALTIMORE, 60.55.1 (once Oxford, Robinson). *Solon to Salamis*, 94, fig. 9; *BABesch*, 17 (1942) 9, fig. 20; *CV* Robinson 1, pl. 37.3; Cambitoglou, *Nicholson Museum*, pl. 27.3–4 (parts); Shapiro, *Tyrants*, pl. 29F; Williams, *Johns Hopkins*, 161–162, no. 109.

255.17 BERLIN, 30852. *Para* 260; *BAdd* 130.

255.19, pl. 44.4A–C OXFORD, 1889.1011 (V 247). *Apollo*, 117 (April 1983) 277, fig. 3; Boardman, *ABFV*, fig. 250; Carpenter, *Art and Myth*, fig. 63 (part); *LIMC*, VII, pl. 365, Poseidon 156 (BD); Simon, *Götter*, 84, fig. 80 (part); Rizza, *Sicilia*, I, 184, fig. 2 (part); *Ta Attika*, 291.38ter (part).

255.20 ATHENS, 18567 (E 1836) (once Empedokles). *ABV* 522; *Acta Archaeologica*, 57 (1986) 9, fig. 8 (drawing); Delavaud-Roux, *Danses Armées*, 161, no. 58 (part); Hedreen, *Silens*, pl. 36 (parts); *LIMC*, VIII, pl. 768, Silenoi 130 (part of BD).

255.22 TARANTO, 14385. *Taranto* I.3, 261, no. 66.1 (part).

255.23 LONDON, B 576. *ABV* 480.

255.26 NEW HAVEN, 1913.112 (112) (once Stoddard). Burke & Pollitt, 36–37, no. 36; *Fest Bakalakis*, pl. 23.3–4; *LIMC*, VIII, pl. 391, Hippokampos 4; *Museum Helveticum*, 40 (1983) 150, fig. 6 (drawing).

255.27 LONDON, 1920.3–15.1. *Etudes de Lettres*, 1983 (4) 47, fig. 15 (part); *Jb*, 103 (1988) 73, fig. 5. Kurtz, *AWL*, pl. 60.1.

255.28 BERLIN, 3252. *ABV* 522; Boardman, *ABFV*, fig. 251 (part); Shapiro, *Personifications*, 141, fig. 95 (part); Recke, *Gewalt*, pl. 42c; *Hephaistos*, 21/22 (2003/04) 58, fig. 2 (drawing).

255.29, pl. 46.1 BERLIN, not known where, 3253. *Berard, Image* 203, fig. 3 (part); Ducrey, *Guerre*, 238 (drawing of part).

255.30, pl. 45.4a–b NEW YORK, 07.286.68. *ABV* 522; *Para* 260; *LIMC*, IV, pl. 127, Gigantes 202 (parts); *LIMC*, V, pl. 267, Hermes 829 (part).

255.33 PALERMO, 1888. *LIMC*, IV, pl. 133, Gigantes 258E (part).

256.34 BUFFALO, 33.135 (G 479) (once Roman market). *ABV* 522; Neils, *Goddess and Polis*, 18, 182, no. 55; Shapiro, *Tyrants*, pl. 15A (part); Nick, *Parthenos*, pl.12.2 (part).

256.35 TARANTO, 4421. *Taranto* I.3, 309, no. 92.1 (parts).

256.36 PRINCETON, 1952.47 (once New York, 06.1021.73). *ABV* 522; *LIMC*, VII, pl. 706, Kyknos I 117 (parts).

256.37 TARANTO, 4418. *Taranto* I.3, 309, no. 91.1 (part).

256.38, 157 ATHENS, Acr., 2339. *Acta Upsaliensis* 2 (1978) 68, fig. 1.

256.46 LONDON, Christie's (once Northwick, Spencer-Churchill). *Para* 260.

256.48, pl. 45.5 (part) LONDON, B 651. Buschor, *Jenseits*, 59, fig. 46; *BMY*, 4 (1980) 70, fig. 36; Hornbostel, *Kropatscheck*, 109, left (part).

256.49, 147, pl. 45.6 (S) ATHENS, 1133; *BAdd* 130; *Jb*, 99 (1984) 17, fig. 9 (drawing); *Para* 260; Touchefeu-Meynier, *Thèmes Odysséens*, pl. 14.3; Andreae, *Ulisse*, 53, fig. 13 (drawing).

256.50, 150, 155, pl. 47.3 ATHENS, 1132 (CC 957). *ABV* 522; *Para* 260; *BAdd* 130; Brommer, *Heracles*, pl. 42 (part); Immerwahr, *Attic Script* pl. 25.107 (part); *Jb* 115 (2000) 68, fig. 6 (parts).

256.52 VIENNA, 197 (once Lamberg). Galinsky, *Herakles Theme*, pl. 4, fig. 6.

256.53 VIENNA, 1841. *ABV* 522; Brommer, *Heracles,* 27, fig. 7 (drawing); *LIMC*, V, pl. 71, Herakles 2245 (part); *Ta Attika*, 292.F40 (parts of BD).

257.56 TARANTO, 4573. *BCH*, 92 (1968) 569, figs. 17–18; Delavaud-Roux, *Danses Armées*, 77, no. 6; Lippolis, *Eroi*, 15, 32, 56, figs. 4, 22, 46 (parts, including colour); *Taranto* I.3, 5, 50, 154, no. 9.1 (parts, colour of part).

257.57 TARANTO, 4420. *Taranto* I.3, 309, no. 90.1 (parts).

257.60 PRINCETON (once New York, 06.1021.72). *ABV* 704; *Para* 260.

257.61, pl. 46.2A–B PALERMO, 2788. *ABV* 522.

257.63 TARANTO, 6832 (2033). *StudAnt*, 8.1 (1995) 17, fig. 3 (BD); Semeraro, *Salento arcaico*, 113, FIG. 63 (part).

257.65 VIENNA, 86. *ABV* 522.

257.66 PARIS, CabMéd, 300 (once Oppermann, 47. *CV* 2, pl. 85.6–8.

257.67 VIENNA, 195. *ABV* 522; Bernhard-Walcher, *Antikes Leben,* 65, no.16 (BD).

257.68, pl. 48.2 (part) BARI, 2732. Hornbostel, *Kropatscheck,* 109, right (part).

257.71, 150, 151 ATHENS, 1158 (CC 1002). Cambitoglou, *Nicholson Museum,* pl. 27.1 (part).

257.72 NEW YORK, 41.162.146 (once Gallatin). *ABV* 522, 704; *BAdd* 130; Schnapp, *Chasseur,* 217, fig. 87 (parts of BD); Bonacasa, *Stile Severo,* pl. 4.2 (drawing).

257.73, 110, 149, 157, pl. 47.2 (part) ATHENS, 1138 (CC 959). *Etudes de Lettres,* 1983 (4) 41, fig. 3 (part); *LIMC,* II, pl. 767, Athena 579; Shapiro, *Tyrants,* pl. 10; *Studies Oswald,* 218, fig. 3 (part).

257.74 KANSAS CITY, 34.289. *Para* 260; Shapiro, *Tyrants,* pl. 11a–b.

257.75, 148, 157, pl. 45.2 (part) DRESDEN, ZV 1700. *BullMich,* 9 (1989–91) 36, fig. 6 (part); *Para* 262.

257.76 PARIS, Cab Méd, H 2985. *CV* 2, pl. 84.5–6.

257.77 NEW YORK (N.Y.), private (once Geneva, Hirsch). *Para* 260.

257.79 KARLSRUHE, B 27 (186). *ABV* 522; *CV* 1, pl. 13.1–2; Knittlmayer, *Demokratie,* pl. 18.2–3 (parts of BD); *LIMC,* I, Achilleus 221 (not illustrated).

257.80 GOTHA, ZV 897. *Para* 260; *CV* 1, pl. 39.3–5.

257.82 COPENHAGEN, 8759. Aktseli, *Altäre,* pl. 1.1 (part); *Para* 260.

257.84 BRUSSELS, A 2295. *CV* 2, pl. 1 (62).5.

258.86 GELA, N 26; *BAdd* 130; *Para* 260; *Ta Attika,* 292.F41 (parts of BD).

258.87 PARIS, CabMed, 298. *ABV* 522; *Para* 260; *BAdd* 130; Berard, *Anodoi,* 6, figs. 21–22; *BABesch,* 64 (1989) 15, fig. 12 (drawing of part); *Fest Himmelmann,* pl. 34.5–6.

258.88 BERLIN F 2000. *LIMC* I, 326, Aias 75 (drawing).

258.90 NEW YORK, 06.1021.75. *BCH,* 92 (1968) 570, fig. 19; Delavaud-Roux, *Danses Armées,* 79, no. 8 (part).

258.98 PALAZZOLO ACREIDE, 2628. *ABV* 522.

258.99 NAPLES, 126006. *ABV* 704.

258.100 NAPLES, 11. *ABV* 704.

258.104, 111, 153–154, 157 ATHENS, 1809 (CC 1025). *ARV²* 689.4; *BAdd* 280; *Fest Bakalakis,* pl. 24 (including drawing).

258.105 NEW YORK, 08.258.28. *ARV²* 690.7; *BAdd* 280; Mertens, *White Ground,* pl. 37.3 (part).

258.106 PARIS, CabMed, 299. *ARV²* 690.11, 704.

258.106TER MARBURG, 1900. *BAdd* 130. *Para* 260; *BullMich,* 9 (1989–91) 37, fig. 7 (part).

259.108 BRUSSELS, A 3131. *ABV* 523; *ARV²* 682.107; *BAdd* 279.

259.109 BRUSSELS, A 3132. *ABV* 523; *ARV²* 681.91; *BAdd* 279; Cavalier, *Silence et Fureur,* 344, fig. 144 (part).

259.110 OXFORD, 226 (225). *ABV* 527.25; *BAdd* 131. *Para* 264; Recke, *Gewalt,* pl. 55c.

259.111 CAMBRIDGE, GR 8.1937 (37.8). *ABV* 526.1; *BAdd* 131; *CV* 2, pl. 2.3; Darracott, *Ricketts and Shannon,* no. 56.

259.112 FRANKFURT, MusVF, β 306 (307) (1941.9). *ABV* 530.72; *Para* 260.112, 264.72; Nick, *Parthenos,* pl.6.4 (BD).

259.113 LONDON, 1928.1–17.46. *ABV* 527.29, 535.7.

259.114 VIENNA, 760. *ABV* 531.4.

259.115 THEBES, 17077 (R.46.83). *ABV* 530.70; *BAdd* 132; Thöne, *Nike,* pl. 3.1 (drawing of BD); *CV,* pl. 70.

259.116 LONDON, B 623. *ABV* 531.8.

259.117 LONDON, B 624. *ABV* 531.11.

259.118 PARIS, F 472. *ABV* 528.45.

259.119, pl. 45.1 BERLIN, not known where, F 4003. *ARV²* 532.1.

259.120 LONDON, 1864.10–7.237. *ABV* 531.5; *BAdd* 132; Delavaud-Roux, *Danses Armées,* 100, no. 26 (part); Ceccarelli, *Pirrica,* pl. 3.3 (BD).

259.121 LONDON, 1864.10–7.243. *ABV* 531.9; *BAdd* 132.

259.122 ATHENS, 1085 (CC 772). *ABV* 535.15,528.40; *BAdd* 133.

259.123 BRUSSELS, R 315. *ABV* 535.16, 528.41; *BAdd* 133; *LIMC,* VIII, pl. 671, Polyphemos I 43 (BD).

259.124 PARIS, A 482. *ABV* 535.14, 528.39; *Para* 267; *BAdd* 133.

259.125 LONDON, 1894.11–1.289. *ABV* 535.17, 528.42; *BAdd* 133.

260.126 LONDON, 1864.10–7.228 (B 502). *ABV* 535.13, 528.38; *BAdd* 133; *LIMC*, VIII, pl. 671, Polyphemos I 44 (BD); Andreae, *Ulisse,* 131, no. 2.21 (colour).

260.128, pl. 45.3 BERLIN, F 1933. *ABV* 532.2; *BAdd* 132.

260.129 BOSTON, 98.924. *ABV* 524.1; *BAdd* 131; *Ktema,* 15 (1990) pl. 4.4 at p. 155 (part); *LIMC*, V, pl. 112, Herakles 2834; *Stips Votiva,* 9, fig. 1 (part).

260.130 LONDON, B 618. *ABV* 525.2.

260.131 LONDON, B 617. *ABV* 525.3; *Para* 263.

260.132 UNKNOWN (once Naples, Hamilton). *ABV* 525.

260.133 PARIS, F 372. *ABV* 531.1; *BAdd* 132.

260.134 LONDON, B 627. *ABV* 531.2.

260.135 LONDON, 1864.10–7.222 (B 628). *ABV* 531.3; *BAdd* 132; Kephalidou, *Nikitis,* pl. 54 (part); Nick, *Parthenos,* pl. 14.5 (drawing).

260.136 LONDON, 1864.10–7.248 (B 626). *ABV* 531.4; *BAdd* 132.

260.138 PARIS, MusRodin, 232.247 (232). *ABV* 530.85; *BAdd* 132.

260.139 LONDON, B 622. *ABV* 525.3.

260.140 PARIS, CabMéd, 270. *ABV* 531.7.

260.141 PARIS, CabMéd, 272. *ABV* 531.6; *BAdd* 132; Delavaud-Roux, *Danses Armées,* 78, no. 7 (part).

APPENDIX XVbis

OINOCHOAI FROM THE WORKSHOP OF THE ATHENA PAINTER

260.1 LOST (once BERLIN, F 1934). *ABV* 528.44; *BAdd* 131; *Kernos,* 2 (1989) 81, fig. 2A (part); *LIMC*, VI, pl. 90, Lamia 1.

260.2 ROME, 5311. *ABV* 531.2.

260.3 FRANKFURT, MusVF, β 307. *ABV* 528.46; *BAdd* 132. *Para* 264.

260.4 OXFORD, 230. *ABV* 529.53.

260.5 COMPIEGNE, 1009. *ABV* 529.54.

261.7 OXFORD, 229. *ABV* 530.77.

261.8 PARIS, Market. *ABV* 531.3.

261.9 VORONEZH, 101 (once Tartu). *ABV* 527.18.

261.10 COPENHAGEN, Ny Carlsberg, 2673. *ABV* 526.1.

261.11 COMPIEGNE, 1032. *ABV* 527.13.

261.12 PARIS, Market. *ABV* 531.1.

261.13 LONDON, 1867.5–8.942. *ABV* 531.12; *BAdd* 132.

261.14 PARIS, CabMed, 273. *ABV* 527.16.

261.15 PARIS, CabMed, 274. *ABV* 530.69; *Para* 264.

261.16 NAPLES, RC 203. *ABV* 529.64.

261.17 LONDON, B 629. *ABV* 530.82.

261.18 FRANKFURT, Schaeffer. *ABV* 526.5, 533.1.

261.19 LONDON, B 511. *ABV* 526.6, 534.2.

261.20 LONDON, B 512. *ABV* 526.7, 534.3.

261.21 LECCE, 563. *ABV* 449.6, 527.15; *Para* 264; Semeraro, *Salento arcaico*, 87–88, figs. 43, 45.147 (BD, profile).

261.22 LONDON, 1864.10–7.9. *ABV* 527.20; *BAdd* 131; *LIMC*, VIII, pl. 525, Mainades 6 (part of BD).

261.23 LECCE, 562. *ABV* 530.78, 534.7; *Para* 264, 266.

261.24 LONDON, B 520. *ABV* 530.68, 534.4.

261.25 NEW YORK, 06.1021.76. *ABV* 529.66.

261.26 LONDON, B 500. *ABV* 528.37, 535.12.

261.27 TÜBINGEN, S/10.717 (D 61). *ABV* 535.5, 527.26; *BAdd* 133; Kimmig, *Heuneburg*, pl. 22.4 (part).

261.28 BRUSSELS, A 261. *ABV* 530.79, 534.8.

261.29 PARIS, F 354. *ABV* 529.59.

261.30 LEIDEN, PC V45 (II.1694, XVII.A1). *ABV* 525.4; *BAdd* 131.

261.31 BERLIN, F 1937. *ABV* 525.5, 704; *BAdd* 131; *CV* 7, pls. 33.2–4, 48.7, BEILAGE H (including profile).

261.32 SÈVRES, 2035. *ABV* 525.6, 704; *BAdd* 131; Grabow, *Schlangenbilder*, pl. 23.K108 (parts).

261.33 BRUSSELS, BibRoy, 6. *ABV* 525.7; *BAdd* 131.

261.34 LONDON, B 619. *ABV* 525.8.

261.35 OXFORD, 1879.147 (V 228). *ABV* 525.9.

LEKYTHOI IN THE MANNER OF THE ATHENA PAINTER

With plain black body, from his workshop:

262.6 RHODES, 12906. *ARV²* 693.8.

Two lekythoi with the picture confined to the shoulder, by one hand:

262.1 OXFORD, 1889.1013 (V 251). Anderson, *Hunting,* 50, fig. 18 (S); *Cité des Images,* 59, fig. 88 (S); Kurtz, *AWL,* pl. 67.4; Schnapp, *Chasseur* 222, no. 99 (S); *Ta Attika,* 293.F47 (part of S).

Four lekythoi with rf. shoulder-decoration by one hand:

262.1, pl. 22.2 LONDON, E 573. *ARV²* 694; *BAdd* 280; *Antike Kunst,* 16 (1973) pl. 7.2; Delavaud-Roux, *Danses Armées,* 82, no.11.

262.2 PALERMO, 2792. *ABV* 523; *BAdd* 130.

262.4 LONDON, 1863.7–28.451. *ARV²* 1666.

Three lekythoi in 'semi-outline', by one hand:

262.1 NAPLES, 81267 (H 2438). *ARV²* 689.1.

262.3 BERLIN, F 2250. *ARV²* 689.3; *Ausgestellte Werke,* 114, no. 6 (part).

BEAZLEY'S ATTRIBUTIONS TO THE ATHENA PAINTER

523.7 HAVANA, P 141. Olmos, *Habana,* 145, no. 62.

523.10 HAVANA, P 144. Olmos, *Habana,* 148, no. 65; Olmos, *Lagunillas,* 96, no.26.

(523) BASEL, market (once H. Cahn). *Para* 261; *H.A.C, Kunst der Antike, Basel,* June 2002, 3 (colour of parts); *Jean David Cahn AG Basel,* Auktionen, 3, 18.10.2002, 14–15, no. 26 (colour of parts).

(523) AMSTERDAM, 3737. *Para* 261; *Stips Votiva,* 87, fig. 7.

(523) BASEL, Cahn, HC 909. *Para* 261; Cambitoglou, *Nicholson Museum,* pl. 27.2; Kreuzer, *Frühe Zeichner,* no. 122.

(523) RIEHEN, private (once Luzern, market). *Para* 261; *BAdd* 131; Delavaud-Roux, *Danses Armées,* 92, no.19 (part).

(523) BLOOMINGTON, 65.66 (once Switzerland, private). *Para* 161; *BAdd* 131; *Jb.* 115 (2000) 27, fig. 25 (parts); *LIMC,* VIII, pl. 738, Seirenes 67 (part).

(523) BASEL, market. *Para* 262, 263; Berard, *Images,* 126, fig. 9 (parts).

(523) GELA, 14. *Para* 261; *Ta Attika,* 293.F46 (part).

GROUP OF THE ATHENA PAINTER

524.1 BONN, 340. Schäfer, *Symposium*, pl. 46.1–2 (parts).

525.2 EDINBURGH, 1956.433 (224.375). *CV*, pl. 12.1–3.

525.10 ROME, Capitolini, 51. *Para* 263; *LIMC*, V, pl. 215, Hermes 160.

526.2 WARSAW, 142453 (once Goluchow). *Para* 263; *LIMC*, VIII, pl. 10, Thetis 16 (BD).

526.9, 534.2 BERLIN, F 1932. *BAdd* 133; *CV*, 7, pl. 35.1–2, Beilage H.

526.2 TARANTO, 20322. *BAdd* 131; D'Amicis, *Taranto* I.3, 301, no. 81.49.

527.12 CAPUA, 149. *CV*, 2, pl. 8.6–7.

527.17 SARASOTA, 1600.G5 (once London, Sotheby's). *Para* 264; *BAdd* 131; Carpenter, *Fifth-Century Imagery*, pl. 17a.

527.28 BOLOGNA, 73. *LIMC*, V, pl. 77, Herakles 2336.

528.33 HAMBURG, 1899.98. *BAdd* 131; *LIMC*, V, pl. 93, Herakles 2568.

528.34 ARMONK (once Scarsdale (NY), Private). *Para* 264; Wolf, *Herakles*, fig. 120.

528.43 PARIS, Cab.Med., 268. *BAdd* 131; *DialHist*, 10 (1989) 233, fig. 22; *Revue du Nord*, 68 (January–March 1986) 25, fig. 5 (drawing).

528.47 CAMBRIDGE (MA), 1927.154. *BAdd* 132; *LIMC*, IV, pl. 138, Gigantes 295.

530.80 FERRRARA, 296 (T 125). *Para* 264; Berti and Guzzo, 275, no.142.

(531) FERRARA, 16338 (T 57 D VP). *Para* 265; *BAdd* 132; Berti and Restani, 56.

(531) UNIVERSITY, 1977.3.73. *Para* 265; *BAdd* 132; *LIMC*, IV, pl. 35, Europe I 34.

APPENDIX XVI

VASES BY THE EMPORION PAINTER

263.1 BARCELONA, 383 (once Gerona). *ABV* 584.1; *BAdd* 138; *Arte Griego*, 24–25, figs. 17–19.

263.2 UNKNOWN (once Barcelona, Montaner). *ABV* 584.2.

263.4 PARIS, CabMéd, 312 (once Oppermann, 105). *CV* 2, pl. 81.3–5; Frontisi-Ducroux and Vernant, pl. 22 (drawing).

263.5 UNKNOWN (once Barcelona, Montaner). *ABV* 584.5.

263.7 PALERMO, 2040. Moret, *Sphinx*, pl. 37.

263.8 GERONA. *ABV* 584.8; *BAdd* 138.

263.10 HEIDELBERG, S 70. *CV* 4, pl. 172.8, 9.

263.11 RHODES, 12149. *CV* Rodi 2, pl. 1 (499) 2, 4; *Clara Rhodos*, IV, 64, figs. 38–39.

263.15 AMSTERDAM, 1636. *CV* Scheurleer 1, pl. 1 (37).2; *Mythen, Mensen en Muziek*, 44, no. 101 (part)

263.16 GENEVA, 10762.1923. *CV* 2, pl. 79.5–8.

263.17, 136 ATHENS, 512. *BCH*, 92 (1968) 563, figs. 12, 13; Delavaud-Roux, *Danses Armées*, 83, no. 12 (parts).

264.24 OXFORD, 1934.67. Kurtz, *AWL*, pl. 72.5.

264.27 PARIS, CabMéd, 303. *ABV* 584.27; *Para* 291.

264.29 OXFORD, 1927.4455. Moret, *Sphinx*, pl. 36.1–2.

264.30 SYRACUSE, 8612. Moret, *Sphinx*, pl. 36.4 (part).

264.31 PARIS, ED 61 (L 39). Kephalidou, *Nikitis*, pl. 62.

264.32 CAMBRIDGE, GR 107.1864 (G 132).

264.34 SAN SIMEON, 9492 (once Athens, market). *ABV* 586.

264.36 EDINBURGH, 1956.451 (L 224.403). *CV* 1, pl. 15.21–23; Wijer, *Polyphemusavontuur*, no. 146 (drawing).

264.37 GELA, 40229 (N 41) (once Navarra). *CV* 3, pls. 23.1–4, 25.5; Lissarrague, *Guerrier*, 27, fig. 3 (drawing); *Ta Attika*, 323.H1 (part of BD); Recke, *Gewalt*, pl. 47b.

264.39, 137, 165–167, pl. 48.4A–B VIENNA, 5247; *BAdd* 138; Cesare, *Statue in Immagine*, 212, fig. 148 (parts); *Etudes de Lettres*, 1983 (4) 30, fig. 20A–B; Mertens, *White Ground*, pl. 38.2 (part); *Para* 291.39.

264.40 MANNHEIM, 128. *Para* 291; Moret, *Sphinx*, 12.1–3.

265.41 PRINCETON, 57. *ABV* 584.41; *BAdd* 138; *LIMC*, VIII, pl. 804, Sphinx 171 (part); Moret, *Sphinx*, 12.4–5.

265.44 CORINTH, T 1696. *Hesperia*, 64 (1995) pl. 95.7 (part).

265.47 LONDON, B 650. Moret, *Sphinx*, pl. 35.1–3.

ALABASTRA, CONNECTED WITH THE EMPORION PAINTER

265.5 SARAJEVO, 655 (88). *CV*, pl. 24.1–2, 4–5.

LEKYTHOI IN HIS STYLE, AND PERHAPS BY HIS HAND

265.3 COMPIEGNE, 1046. *ABV* 585.5.

LEKYTHOI IN HIS MANNER

266.1, 169 ATHENS, 488. *ABV* 586.1; *BAdd* 139; *DdA*, 1988, 1, 115, fig. 1 (part); *Ceramics in Context*, 159, fig. 4.

266.2 PARIS, Market (once Paris, Prof. Dr. S. Pozzi, 454). *ABV* 586.5.

266.3 CAMBRIDGE, GR 81.1864 (G 103). *ABV* 586.6; *BAdd* 139.

XVII. LEKYTHOI BY THE BELDAM PAINTER

266.1, 170–172, 176, 190–191, pls. 49, 50.2, 51.1 ATHENS, 1129. *Para* 292; *AJA*, 86 (1982) pl. 2, fig. 9; *Acta*, 7/8 (1976/77) 262, fig. 20 (drawing); *Annali*, NS 1 (1994) 117, fig. 1 (drawing); Boardman, *ABFV*, fig. 277; Frontisi-Ducroux, *Masque*, pl. 69 (drawing); *Kernos*, 2 (1989) 80, figs. 1A–B (drawing, part); Osborne, *Archaic and Classical*, 191, fig. 116 (part); *LIMC*, VI, pl. 90, Lamia 2 (drawing).

266.2, 51, 172, 173–174, 176, 178, pl. 51.2A–D (S, BD) ATHENS, 12801 (N 973). Brijder, *Proceedings*, 265, fig. 1 (part of BD); Kurtz, *AWL*, pl. 18.1.

266.3, 172, 176, 178, pl. 50.3 ATHENS, 1125 (CC 960). *BAdd* 139; Verbanck-Pierard, *Hippocrate*, 265, no. 34 (BD).

266.4, 172, 176, 179, pl. 53.2 (part) ATHENS, 14858. Schnapp, *Chasseur* 232, no. 145 (drawing of BD).

266.5 ITHACA, Stavros. *ABV* 586.5.

266.6, pls. 50.4, 51.3 (S, part of BD) ATHENS, Ceramicus. ARV² 751; *Para* 292; Kurtz, *AWL*, pl. 70.5.

266.8 COPENHAGEN, 1941. ARV² 751.3.

266.10 NEW HAVEN 1955.4.103, (once Athens, Polytechneion, 3536). *Para* 292; *BAdd* 139; Halm-Tisserant, *Realitès*, pl.3.

267.11, 171, 172–174, 177–178, 180–181, 190, pl. 50.1 ATHENS, 1288 (487, CC 969). Buitron-Oliver, *New Perspectives*, 51, figs. 20–22.

267.12, 171, 173, 175–177, 191, pls. 51.4, 52.1 ATHENS, 1982. ARV² 751.1; *BAdd* 285; Kurtz, *AWL*, pl. 18.2.

267.13, 168, 171, 173, 175–176, pl. 52.2 ATHENS, 1983. ARV² 751; *BAdd* 285.

(b) Smaller lekythoi, with the same proportions as Athens 487, all black-figure

267.14 LONDON, B 648. *Jb* 27 (1912) Beilage I, IV; Bieber, *Theaterwesen,* 89, fig. 92 (drawing); Bieber, *Theater,* 19, fig. 57 (drawing); Stackelberg, pl. 16.1; Lehnstaedt, pl. 4.3 (K 76).

267.15 CORINTH, T 814. *Corinth* XIII, no. 324.4, pl. 95.

(c) Smaller lekythoi with different proportions, all black-figure

267.17 CAMBRIDGE, GR 96.1864 (G 121).

267.19 ERLANGEN, I 429. *LIMC,* VII, pl. 211, Peliades 6D; Meyer, *Medeia,* pl. 7.1 (drawing); Vojatzi, *Argonauten-bilder,* pl. 13.B77 (part).

(d) 'Chimney-lekythoi', all black-figure

267.24 CAMBRIDGE, GR 35.1896 (G 120).

267.25 BRUSSELS, A 2296. *LIMC,* VIII, pl. 612, Pan 5 (part of BD); Marquardt, *Pan,* pl. 28.2.

267.26 VATICAN, 451. *ABV* 586.26.

267.27 VIENNA, 132. *BCH,* 92 (1968) 572, fig. 26; Delavaud-Roux, *Danses Armées,* 87, no. 16 (part).

267.30 CORINTH, T 1570. *Hesperia,* 64 (1995) pl. 91.3 (part).

268.37 CAMBRIDGE, GR 100.1864 (G 125).

268.41 SAN SIMEON, 5661. *Para* 292.

268.43 PARIS, CA 2525; *BAdd* 139; *Para* 292.

268.44 ZURICH, 2493 (once Basel, Pfuhl). *CV* I, pl. 19.22–25; *LIMC,* V, pl. 568, Kaineus 28 (part).

268.45, 178, pl. 53.6 ATHENS, 610 (CC 1012). Laufer, *Kaineus,* pl. 8, figs. 23.1–2 (part, drawing).

268.46 LONDON, B 649. *BCH,* 92 (1968) 572, fig. 28; Delavaud-Roux, *Danses Armées,* 86, no. 15 (part); Ceccarelli, *Pirrica,* pl. 4.1 (BD).

268.48 NEW YORK, Sotheby's (once Boston, 93.101). Wolf, *Herakles,* figs. 123–124; *SothPB,* 12.6.2001, 156–157, 169, no.259 (part).

268.52 CORINTH, T 566.118. Kurtz, *AWL,* pl. 70.8.

268.53 UTRECHT. *ABV* 586.53.

268.54, 178, 179, pl. 54.2 ATHENS, 1061. Kerenyi, *Dionysos,* fig. 30 (drawing); *Para* 292.

268.55 ST. PETERSBURG, 146; *BAdd* 139; *Para* 292.

268.56, 178, pl. 53.5A–B ATHENS, 599 (CC 890). Boardman, *ABFV*, fig. 278.1, 2; *DialHist* 10 (1984) 235, fig. 27; *LIMC*, VII, pl. 210, Peliades 6A (parts); Meyer, *Medeia*, pl. 4.2–3; Vojatzi, *Argonautenbilder*, pl. 13.B78.

269.57 ATHENS, E 1556 (once Empedokles). *ABV* 585.57.

269.58 ATHENS, 12805. *LIMC*, VII, pl. 211, Peliades 6C; Meyer, *Medeia*, pl. 6.1–3.

269.62 CAMBRIDGE, GR 60.1864 (G 83). *CV* 1, pl. 22.24.

269.64 ATHENS, 597 (CC 893). *ABV* 586.64.

269.66, 178–179, pl. 54.1 ATHENS, 548 (CC 884). *Para* 292.66.

269.67 LONDON, B 658. *ABV* 586.67; *BABesch*, 64 (1989) pl. 1B; *GVGetty* 2 (1985) 112, fig. 21.

269.69 PARIS, CabMed, 292. *Para* 293.

269.70 SAN SIMEON. *ABV* 586.70.

269.71 CORINTH, T 759. *Para* 292.

269.73, 185 KARLSRUHE, B 310 (189). *CV* 1, pl. 32.2.

(e) A smallish lekythos in outline, perhaps by the Beldam painter, and certainly from his workshop

269.73BIS CORINTH, MP 90. *ABV* 752.

XVIIIbis. GROUPS OF VASES NEAR THE BELDAM PAINTER

(α) LEKYTHOI – IN OUTLINE – BY THE PAINTER of LONDON D 65

Large:

270.1 PARIS, Market (Feuardent). *ARV²* 752.1.

270.2 LONDON, D 65. *ARV²* 752.2; *BAdd* 285; *Annali*, 10 (1988) fig. 15.1(part); Buxton, *Grèce imaginaire*, pl. 4A (part).

Small:

270.3 UTRECHT, H 16. *ARV²* 753.1.

270.4, 175, 180 ATHENS, 12750 (N 1007). *ARV²* 753.2; *Annali*, 10 (1988) fig. 25.4 (drawing).

ADDENDA TO BEAZLEY'S ATTRIBUTIONS TO THE BELDAM PAINTER

572.7 PARIS, CabMed, 306. *Para* 294; *BAdd* 137; Grabow, *Schlangenbilder*, pl. 18.K84 (drawing); *Ktema*, 15 (1990) pl. 4.1–2 at p. 154 (parts); *LIMC*, VII, pl. 489, Python 3 (part).

587.1 ATHENS, 16350. *Para* 292; *BAdd* 139; Shapiro, *Personifications*, 153, fig. 113 (part).

(587.5BIS) 709 AMIENS 3057.310 (623). *BAdd* 139; Drivaud, *Amiens*, 89, no.32 (part).

(587) ATHENS, Agora, P 10319. *Para* 293; *BCH*, 92 (1968) 572, fig. 27; *Hesperia*, 32 (1963) pl. 37.B1; Delavaud-Roux, *Danses Armées*, 95, no.21 (part).

(587) OXFORD, 1956.945. *Para* 293; Ceccarelli, *Pirrica*, pl. 4.2 (BD).

(587) HOBART, 38. *Para* 294; *LIMC*, VI, pl. 136, Leto 56.

(587) BERGEN, VK 62.115. *Para* 294; *LIMC*, VI, pl. 132, Leto 29b (part).

(β) SMALL LEKYTHOI IN SILHOUETTE-TECHNIQUE

270.4 CAMBRIDGE, GR 61.1864 (G 84). *CV* 1, pl. 22.9.

(γ) THE ICARUS PAINTER

Lekythoi

Red-figure:

270.1 NEW YORK, 24.97.37. *ARV²* 696.1, 1666; *BAdd* 280;

270.2 PROVIDENCE, 25.084. *ARV²* 697.18; *BAdd* 280.

270.3 PARIS, L 52. *ARV²* 697.19; *BAdd* 280; Lissarrague, *Guerrier*, 212, fig. 119 (drawing).

270.4 ROME, 50582. *ARV²* 697.23, 1666; *BAdd* 281.

270.5 SÈVRES, 2038. *ARV²* 697.5.

271.6 WÜRZBURG, L 549. *ARV²* 698.48.

271.7 COPENHAGEN, 137 (VIII 949). *ARV²* 698.32; *BAdd* 281; Christiansen, *Rediscovery*, 106, no.162 (colour of part).

271.8 ATHENS, 1346 (CC 1472). *ARV²* 698.33.

271.9 ATHENS, 1504 (CC 1475). *ARV²* 698.34.

271.10 FRANKFURT, LHaus. *ARV²* 699.60.

271.11 LONDON, E 613. *ARV²* 699.61; *BICS*, 35 (1988) pl. 10.

Outline:

271.12 PARIS, F 375. *ARV²* 699.66.

271.13 ATHENS, Vlasto. *ARV²* 699.63.

271.14 COPENHAGEN, 133 (VIII 30). *ARV²* 699.67.

271.15, pl. 54.5 (part) ATHENS, Vlasto. *ARV²* 699.65.

271.16 GOLUCHOW, 91. *ARV²* 699.75.

Oinochoe (Beazley shape III; red-figure)

271.17 ATHENS, Vlasto. *ARV²* 700.83; *BAdd* 281; *LIMC*, VIII, pl. 399, Hypnos 6 (BD).

Loutrophoros (red-figure)

271.18 LOUVAIN. *ARV²* 700.85.

ADDENDA TO BEAZLEY'S ATTRIBUTIONS TO THE ICARUS PAINTER

697.28 NAPLES, 81605 (H 3216). *LIMC*, VI, pl. 570, Nike 110.

698.37 PARIS, CA 2567. Duby and Perrot, *Femmes*, 207, fig. 29.

698.46 LONDON, E 606. *BICS*, 35 (1988) pl. 1C.

698.47 ATHENS, Agora, P 17601. *Agora*, 30, pl. 88.864 (part).

699.77 LONDON, D 46. *BAdd* 281; *BICS*, 35 (1988) pl. 2D (part).

700.81 NAPLES, 86380 (RC 695). *CV* 5, pls. 72.1–3, 75.12.

700.82 OXFORD, 1947.113. *BICS*, 35 (1988) pl. 2A–C LEFT.

700.84 OXFORD, 1927.4467. *BAdd* 281; *BICS*, 35 (1988) pl. 2A–C RIGHT.

701.10 LEIPZIG, T 429. *BAdd* 281; Paul, *Meisterwerke*, 10, no. 16 (colour of part); Vanhove, *Sport*, 168, no. 20 (colour of part).

701.12 ATHENS, Agora, P 16550. *Agora*, 30, pl. 90.900.

701.15 CAMBRIDGE, GR 5.1929 (29.5). Vanhove, *Sport*, 20, fig. 2.

Index of Collections